THE

CONFESSIONS

OF A

FREE-THINKER.

BY CHARLES SOUTHWELL.

LONDON:

PRINTED FOR THE AUTHOR.

Price One Shilling.

CONFESSIONS

OF

A FREE-THINKER.

INTRODUCTORY CHAPTER.

AFTER ten years of public life the idea of writing these Confessions suddenly occurred to me. The circumstance to which that idea owed its birth it is desirable should be known. During my long, fierce, bold, and until lately uncompromising opposition to established notions with regard to religion many enemies were raised up, who, if unable to vanquish me in *argument* were perfect masters of *calumny* which they heaped upon my devoted head without stint or measure. From these Confessions it will appear that some of the worst things they have said against me are perfectly true, but this comparatively small amount of truth is so overlaid and disfigured by falsehood that from both or either no other than a distorted view of my character can be obtained. Hence the wide difference of opinion between friends and enemies, between those who know me from personal intercourse and those who know me through the reports of others far more malignant and almost as ignorant as themselves.

Sensitive to *calumny* though despising the *calumniator*, and painfully alive to the many errors of my past life I have often smiled when credited with virtues I never possessed and glowed with indignation when charged with vices my soul loathed and the commission of which never entered into my imagination.

Many public men lay claim to disinterestedness in the advocacy of opinions. I never did. I scorned and do scorn to be thought better than I am. But neither would I be thought worse. Let me here declare that for me posthumous fame has no charms. With the Pizzarro of Kotzebue I can say and say in perfect sincerity, the fame I value shall uplift my *living* estimation, overbear with popular support the envy of my foes, advance my purposes and aid my power. Naturally suspicious of those who preach a contrary doctrine I consider them either dreamers or knaves. To defend this opinion is neither my present business nor intention; my object in these papers being *nothing else than* to exhibit myself mentally and morally (for of my person little need be said, as all who choose may *see* it) as I have been and am without the extenuation of faults or setting down of ought but rigid unmixed truth.

In attempting this which many will think a hopeless task and idle as hopeless, though every statement will be true and a genuine reflection of my own mental state, persons of either sex with whom during my past life I have had associations, tender or otherwise, will not for obvious reasons, appear in these Confessions under the names they bear or have borne. But though names may be false all the facts will be true and it is with facts not names the reader has to deal. Were it otherwise, I should shrink from gratifying a prurient curiosity by laying bare family secrets, or wounding the delicacy and honorable pride, whether of families or individuals. I do what I will with my own reputation; I feel myself warranted in doing so, but no one can be warranted in torturing, or wantonly sporting with, the feelings of others. For these reasons then, if no others, these Confessions will not give the real names of persons, except where I am fully satisfied there is no occasion to suppress them.

Probably what I propose to do, will all be laid to the account of sheerest and most senseless egotism. Well be it so—the reader shall judge. But I feel and am bound to say it, the reader's judgment whether favorable or unfavorable will not disturb me in the least. Perhaps a sentence seemingly so egotistic and harsh would have been better if preceded by some such observation as that of the Irish orator who commenced a speech to his countrymen by saying, " I am going to

insult ye but don't be offended." Without the least
disposition to insult readers of the *Beacon*, sincerity
requires the avowal that if by a truthful exposition
of my thoughts, I should " insult" those kind friends
I desire to honor, it is hoped they will not be
"offended." All crimes and follies notwithstanding, I
can afford to keep a conscience, which conscience like
a true tyrant, leaves me neither rest nor peace till its
commands are obeyed. One of these is to write and
publish a full and candid confession of such circumstances in my past chequered, strange, and stormy life,
as may tend to the glory of truth ; and when I am in
the tomb, shield my memory from the calumniator.
Though still ranked amongst young men Death, who
must come when he will come, may think proper to
make my lease of life a short one. Lest such be the
grim despot's determination, and lest circumstances
should hereafter be less favourable for their publication, I have thought it prudent to publish these
Confessions now.

About the style of them I am not very anxious—my
conviction however is that no other hand could sketch
them so well as my own, because no other mind can
comprehend mine so well as it is comprehended by
itself. No man, observes a modern author, can give
so true a picture of the mind of another as that mind
will infallibly give of itself, whatever disguise may be
attempted. But in my case there is no known motive
for either witholding, distorting, or disguising truth.
Childless, wifeless, without relatives, who can at all be
injured by the sincerest course of action I may resolve to pursue, hypocrisy is unnecessary and would
be the most wanton of wickedness. At the same time
these Confessions will be as remote from whatever is
indecent, or likely to shock the really modest and good,
as is the sky from the earth. Truths, some of which
are startling even to myself, will be presented in all
their nakedness, yet he or she who shall suppose them
outrages upon what is most pure and modest would
commit the same mistake as one who should perceive
no difference between the nakedness of an uncorrupted
savage and that of some shameless wanton.

I have heard of a young female so exquisitely modest
that naked truth, which of all naked things is least
indecent, shocked her so much that she could not even

endure its being mentioned. If among readers of these Confessions, are to be found persons who plume themselves on a modesty like this, my advice is that they attempt not their perusal, as the truths of which they are composed derive more than half their value and all their charm from the simple undisguised nakedness of the form wherein they appear.

The reader who expects from me the burning eloquence which has immortalised the pages of Rousseau, or the poetic fervor that breathes in every line of Lamartine, will be disappointed. In the Confessions of the one and Confidences of the other are strokes of genius that had I the will Nature has denied me the power to rival. Mere imitation is my aversion, and, like the great painter of an age long past, I would rather be a bad original than a good copy. My tale is a simple one and shall be told in a manner plain and unvarnished. No one need fear my reaching the excellence of Saint Augustine, who

> In his fine confessions,
> Makes the reader envy his transgressions.

None will envy *my* transgressions in consequence of any peculiarity in the mode of confessing them, which will, nevertheless, at least have the merit of showing that past errors have been a constant source of uneasiness to me and *only* cause of the bitterest sufferings it has been my lot to experience. Although no convert to the belief that vice has neither its charms nor its pleasures, I am under no alarm lest readers of the *Beacon* may be injured in their morals by certain transgressions I am pledged freely to confess. On the contrary my deliberate conviction is that they will beget in ALL a rooted disgust of whatever is mean, false, deceptive, or cowardly.

SECOND CHAPTER.

EARLY IMPRESSIONS.

" The child is father of the man," and these Confessions would not be complete or answer the purpose of their publication without some account of those impressions which, received at an early period of life, formed, as it were, the nucleus around which have gathered all the thoughts, feelings, joys, sorrows, aspirations, and mortifications, of years long subsequent. What we *are* depends much more upon what we *have been* than is usually supposed ; and great is the mistake of biographers who imagine that the history of childhood is necessarily childish, or that character can be understood without the trouble of watching its early development. Dryden has taught us how the child imposes on the man, and Lord Brougham ventured the bold but well-grounded assertion, that we are recipients of more good, or evil, or both, during the first eight years of life than all the rest put together. To a certainty *my* first eight years of life did go far to determine the course pursued during those which *have* succeeded or *will* succeed.

> 'Tis education forms the infant mind,
> Just as the twig is bent the tree's inclined.

And the reader who takes an interest in while appreciating the object of these Confessions will not deem an impertinent infliction the childish tale a strong sense of what is due to truth requires me to unfold.

My birth was a marvel, having marvellously escaped not being born at all. This odd and rather mysterious " fact" I will explain.

I am the youngest of thirty-three children, all begotten in the regular legal way by one father, who, to borrow a scriptural mode of expression, went in unto three wives, most evidently the last of whom was my mother. She had kindled the flame of love in the breast of my father while residing with him in the capacity of servant. He was a man of powerful mind, and distinguished himself as the improver or creator of several musical instruments. A man who " sought out many inventions" to him we are indebted for the Cabinet Piano Forte, the Upright Grand, the Addition Keys, and those almost forgotten

instruments the Harpsichord and Camrichord. My
recollection of him is shadowy, vague, and therefore
unsatisfactory; but the impression he left upon my
young mind (for he died, alas! before reason had
well ripened within me) was that he belonged to a class
of restless, energetic, determined men, to whose "quick
bosoms quiet is a hell"—a man of temper unceasingly
active and intellect proudly prodigious. From some
cause or other so great was his contempt and hatred of
priests that if by any chance one of the tribe found
his way into the house he would say, " Fanny (my
mother's name was Fanny) *see to the money drawer
and lock up the cupboards.*" "Robbers" was the term he
usually applied to them, and never missed an opportunity to indulge a joke at their expense. Like the
writer of these Confessions, who in this respec
decidedly is " a chip of the old block," he hated with
intensest hatred the pack of hungry wolves who, in
the name of their imaginary *wolf* God, devour the
sheep they profess to guard. On the bed of death,
as in the haunts of life, his haughty soul, like that
of the late Richard Carlile, towered above pigmy
theologians; and how little he dreaded the King of
Terrors was manifest to all who were with him at that
trying hour. He died with a jest in his mouth, for
the lower extremities having mortified some hours
before " the spirit took its flight," and one of the
nurses (an uncommonly nice woman) having tried to
rub life into his dead limbs, he said, with that peculiarly expressive twinkle of the eye I can never
forget, " *Ah, you may do that now, but let me tell you
it would not have been safe to do it a little while ago.*"
But though a Sampson in intellect, like Sampson my
poor father had not always strength enough to resist
temptations spread for him by the fair sex; and the
Bible hero shorn of his locks was not more impotent
than *he* sometimes was under their influence. He
loved woman heartily as every man should, but his
love was not always tempered with discretion. When
upwards of seventy he married my mother (a buxom,
and some who knew her say, handsome lass of twenty),
which to my less courageous intellect appears a bolder
stroke than any prudent person would make for the
handsomest of young wives. " Wives are old men's
nurses," and rather in the capacity of nurse than wife did

my mother act towards my father for many years before
his death.   Up to the period of my birth, and I
believe two or three years after, they cohabited together ; but my birth (though not, like Glo'ster, born
with teeth) cost my mother agonies so acute and distressing that she vowed never again to bear children.
This will in part account for the fact of my not being
weaned till more than three years old.   When full
that age I was as fond of a pull at the sucking bottle
as certain Irish patriots are of " a pull at the Exche-
quer."   Like them, I rarely objected to a pull any
how, any where, or at any time.   If my mother refused, as she frequently did, my pressing importuni-
ties, I watched for an opportunity to pounce upon her,
stool in hand (usually standing to suck), while engaged
in conversation with persons at the door or other
exposed place, and demand " the diddy."   My logic
under such circumstances if not good showed I was a
promising boy.   After teazing with a perseverance
which should have been rewarded by a sound flogging,
I used to say, " *Mother, atn't you a woman?*"   "*Yes.*"
" *Then I'm a man, and must have the diddy.*"   Like
mothers in general, MY mother knew not how to
manage children.   Comparatively illiterate, but full
of kindly feelings, she allowed us to get what is
called " the upper hand" of her.   My rare logic
rarely failed, if not to convince, at least to soften
her ; and so Master Charley got his pull at the sucking bottle.   Weaning me was no joke.   In vain they
said I was sucking all my senses away, for so saying
only had the effect of exciting my juvenile suspicion
that I was more likely to suck all the good things out
of my mother.   At length, however, the tremendous
feat was accomplished, and I began to blush at the
idea of touching the nipple.   I perfectly well remember being taken about a year afterwards by the most
singularly attached of all singular domestics, kind-
hearted old Molly Croker, to the house of a Mrs.
Brannen, who had a child at her breast.   They tried,
but could not persuade me, to have " on the sly" another pull at the sucking bottle , but some fresh-drawn
fluid therefrom being put into a saucer, I compounded
for the sin I was inclined to, and drank it.   Great
was the amusement enjoyed that and many a subsequent night at my expense.   My little brothers and

CONFESSIONS OF A FREE-THINKER.

sisters were never tired of laughing at me; and
smarting severely under a sense of the ridiculous,
the impression upon my mind then was, as it ever
since has been, that putting things in a ridiculous
light is the best mode of making children, whether
young or old, heartily ashamed of them. Another
of the vivid and lasting impressions produced upon
my young senses was consequent upon hearing men
hawk about an account of the execution of Thistle-
wood, surmounted by a wood-cut representing, in true
" Calendar of Horrors" style, a bleeding head separated from the body.   It was the first time I had
been struck by anything of the kind.   Two things
were my special aversion—rats and blood; on either
of which I never could look without a shudder.
" Some men there are," says Shylock, " who love not
a gaping pig; some who are mad when they behold
a cat."   But of the entire animal kingdom the only
creature I ever loathed as well as feared is the rat.
No reasoning can cure me of almost insane fear in
presence of that filthy animal, which accounts, perhaps, for the disgust I feel for *political* rats, who certainly are the more noxious animals of the two.   If
anything, my disgust of cruelty is more intense than
my disgust of these vermin ; and the view of Thistle-
wood's bloody head and mangled limbs impressed
upon my young mind a horror of murder, and more
especially that most deliberate and worst of all murder which, under the sanction of a barbarous law, is
committed on our scaffolds.   Thomas Paine has
beautifully remarked, in reference to certain emotions
he experienced at an early age, on hearing a sermon
every sentence of which suggested ideas of blood and
cruelty, that " the religion which shocks the mind
of a child cannot be true religion."   No juster sentiment ever fell from human lips or distilled from
human pen ; and I declare as my deliberate conviction, that the law whose execution excites horror in
the mind of a child cannot be justice, but authorized
vengeance usurping its sacred name, whilst outraging
its proper functions.   How far the early impression
produced by the accidental circumstance of seeing a
representation and hearing an account of Thistle-
wood's execution has tended to the development
of this conviction I know not, but firmly be-

lieve that it was a circumstance which, though trivial in itself, sufficed to implant within me an undying abhorrence of cruelty, and demonstrates the truth, so poetically expressed by Bulwer, that often the merest trifles will revolutionize all the tides and currents of the heart. Would that a truth so pregnant with usefulness were duly appreciated by all, but more especially by parents, who, with few exceptions, have not the most distant idea of how much, whether of good or evil in the conduct of men, depends upon early impressions. Mine were to a large extent good. My father's contempt for, and my mother's indifference to, every kind or system of superstition secured me from its baneful influence. I was neither forbidden nor commanded to read religious books. My mind—allowed to act in fearless freedom under the guidance of a parent who, though he never discussed religious topics with his children, evidently held all sectarian and systematic religion in utter contempt—grew with my growth and strengthened with my strength. At no time have I professed a supernatural creed or believed a supernatural dogma. My earliest religious impressions had reference to the person of Christ, who was associated in my childish imagination with the idea of a respectable-looking man, in snuff-coloured coat and rays of glory around his head. I also connected him with a certain street in which I often played at *High barbaree* and other games, called Stephen-street, where, strange to say, I thought he lived. The connexion between a snuff-coloured queer-looking coat and the garment without seam worn by the man Jesus a conjurer would be puzzled to discover; but the conceit about the rays of glory around the head is not difficult to be accounted for. I was twelve years old before my opinions on religion assumed a definite shape or tendency. By what circumstances that shape and tendency were determined I propose to relate in the next chapter.

CHAPTER III.

BOYISH REMINISCENCES

In my school days I was remarkable for little else than truant playing and remembering power. A game at cricket or rounders was more to my taste than the dry-as-dust studies so strongly recommended by shallow pedants, who, by forcing the growth of intellect, cripple it for ever. Their error consists in supposing that by loading the memory of children with a heap of words we improve their judging faculty. But to make them *think*, not *talk*, and above all freely and fully to develope their *physical* powers, is the proper business of teachers. After securing a sound body it is time enough to fashion a sound mind. Infant educators are for the most part addle-pated book-worms who mistake *science* for *sense*, and ridiculously imagine that babbling children must be clever, and that capacity to get words by rote is clear evidence of their ability to understand them.

Rousseau in his "Emelius" relates an anecdote illustrative of parental folly in forcing children to learn what they cannot comprehend, and exercising young memory at the cost of judgment. While on a visit at the mansion of a French nobleman he was amazed by the mastery of words displayed by the son and heir, a child about seven years old. The little fellow could talk right on for hours, and to amuse the philosopher guest during this his first visit, was, after dinner, put on the table and told by his admiring parents to entertain him with an account of certain historical transactions. The philosopher listened with astonishment while from the mouth of that precocious genius poured forth what threatened to be a never-ending stream of words. Among other historical incidents referred to was that remarkable one of Alexander and his physician. Readers who are familiar with the life of that hero will remember that when prostrated by illness he received intimation that his most trusted physician had been bribed to poison him. Instead of betraying the least suspicion or alarm, he gave the accusatory letter to the physician with one hand, and, his eyes all the time fixed in calm confidence upon the accused, with the other carried the cup to his lips, and unhesitatingly drank the medicine prescribed. This story the child told so admirably—he seemed so sensibly to feel and appreciate the moral it pointed, that Rousseau was confounded. But afterwards walking in the garden, and busied in reflecting upon what appeared understanding so extraordinary, it occurred to him that the child might not be so profound a thinker as he at first supposed; and shortly after meeting him, he said, " My young friend, what was it that so much excited your admiration in the conduct of Alexander?" " Why," said the child, after some hesitation, " *When mamma made me take physic the other day, I could not help making all sorts of ugly faces, and yet Alexander took a lot of such nasty stuff without making any faces at all.*"

Now, I will venture to say, that of one hundred children who shall be trained, parrot like, to repeat this story about Alexander, *not one* would discover in it a wiser moral than that he was an astonishing hero for drinking filthy physic without making wry faces— a feat no child ever was known to perform. The truth is, " old heads ought not to be expected on young shoulders;" and I believe nothing can be more injurious to *sense* than bothering mere infants with *science*. This conviction may, in part at least, be traced to an early and deep disgust of getting by rote, under fear of punishment, whole pages of (to me) unintelligible gibberish. And yet my memory was prodigious. Of any book that *pleased* me I could, by a single reading, master and retain the leading facts. When under nine years of age I knew more about the *facts* of history than I do now. At that tender age I found no difficulty in beginning at the beginning of history, whether Greek, Roman, Irish, or English, and going right on to the end without omitting in my way a single fact of importance. I could reckon up the monarchs of all civilized nations, and relate all the leading events in which they were concerned. Many a "tuck-in" of eggs and bacon (my favourite dish at that time) have I earned by telling historical tales to dmiring friends and relatives. But my pow er to recollect events has diminished just in the same ratio all my power to judge them has increased. My belief is, thet, generally speaking, people who remember much think little. Men who " talk like a book," from inveterate habit of trusting to memory

rather than inspiration, are seldom profound thinkers
or accurate reasoners.   Certainly I never talked so
well or had such a perfect mastery of fact as when a
child ; yet to reason justly from facts I was unable,
and very much question whether of the many speeches
I made any one was understood by the speaker.   But
his gift of tongue, called by vulgar little boys " gifts
of the gab," being by the same little boys dreaded as
well as admired, I contrived to play dictator amongs
them.   Few of my companions were a match for me
at running, riding, or talking.   Fighting too was an
art on which I piqued myself, but was always willing
to avoid the inconveniences of.   My mother having
allowed me to get the " upper hand" of her, and my
father incapacitated by age from narrowly watching
my movements, I spent much of my time in the streets
where *robbers* most do congregate ; and to ingratiate
myself with these respectable people was part of my
precocious policy.   To this end I used in part to feed
the hungriest and most fightable of them at considerable cost to my cheated parents.   Between an
affectionate mother and pedantic schoolmaster my
young idea had been taught " to shoot" in a most
exraordinary manner.   Envious little boys called me
" cock of the walk," and longed to give me a thr shing
but my little army of hungry retainers were always
ready to reward with a " good licking" any boys of
their own " weight and size" who should say anything
against me.   Nevertheless endless were the scrapes
into which I got, frequently returning home, the hero
of a hard-fought field, with those indubitable evidences of prowess, two black eyes and a bloody nose.
In the meantime my father bitterly complained that I
was running the streets instead of going to school, to
which complaints the poor schoolmaster could say
nothng but   that he had tried severity without effect,
and that though I rarely got to school till an hour after
the other boys were assembled, and frequently did not
show myself there at all, yet *when there* I soon made
up for lost time, and speedily overtook my more
methodical but slow companions.   He was right on
both points.   Flogging never yet did me the least
service, and I believe never will.   No mule ever was
more obstinate than I when treated with severity.   In
my case an ounce of kindness availed and avails more

than tons of punishment. The poor schoolmaster had tried and tried in vain by violence or coercion to subdue my stubborn spirit. Easy to lead, but difficult to drive, he never hit upon the right method of moulding me to his will. Yet he truly told my father that when at school, and inclined to learn, I shot ahead with amazing rapidity. Memory being the faculty most in requisition there, and mine being singularly retentive, the usual class lessons were disposed of without difficulty. But upon the whole, my education was miserably defective. Almost every kind of study was attempted by turns, and none adhered to long. " Plutarch's Lives" was my favorite work, which (out of school) I read with avidity. So great was my admiration of it that after a second reading I from time to time dipped into some one of the " Lives," not so much to refresh memory as delight imagination. I still think them the noblest portraits of the noblest men, and hardly deem exaggerated the estimate of them held by that learned author who said, if all literary works save one were doomed to destruction, and he were called upon to name that one, it would be " Plutarch's Lives." The other books in which I chiefly delighted were Hume and Smollett, " Robertson's History of Charles the Fifth," " Gibbon's Decline and Fall," and accounts of the manners, customs, ceremonies, opinions, and prejudices of the various nations constituting this Bedlam of the Universe. The study of languages, though afterwards a favorite one, was intolerable to me, and like Gibbon, before his studies were bottomed on judgment, and pursued with plan or object, I left school when about half past eleven years, with knowledge enough to puzzle pedants, and ignorance enough to disgrace a Hottentot.' I could boast of little Latin and *no* Greek. At this critical period my father died at the advanced age of eighty eight, and out of respect to his memory I was admitted into the firm of Broadwood and Sons, Piano Forte Manufacturers, where two of my brothers were then employed. They designed to make a Tuner of me; but having got it into my head that working at the bench was more manly and becoming than the lighter and (most people think) genteeler occupation of tuning, I resolved, in a spirit worthy of Sir Pertinax M'Sycophant, to achieve so desirable an object, honestly if I could, *but* to achieve it. Asked by Mr. James Broadwood what I should like to be, my reply was, " A finisher, sir, if you please." " But," said he, " you are neither old nor strong enough to work at a bench, and therefore you had better be a Tuner. "Thank you, sir," rejoined I (the *lie* immediately occurring to me), " but my father always said I had no taste for music, and turning a sow's ear into a silk purse would be no more difficult than to make a Tuner of *me*." He smiled, and without at all suspecting the fraudulent tale my active little brain so readily forged, said, " Well, get one of the men for a master, and set to work as soon as you like."

The strait-laced moralist who is shocked by this Confession may perhaps be comforted by the assurance, that no other lie I ever told has caused me bitterer remorse or keener suffering than this. Though invented for no malicious purpose but the sole one of securing a profession agreeable to my feelings, it resulted in years of misery and utter disgust of life. I soon found that flogging away at a bench, covered with sweat and dust, did not suit me. There were times when to escape the detested trade I would have dared anything, and as will be shown in a subsequent Chapter (patience being exhausted) I did dare much.

Here it is necessary to relate a circumstance which, immediately after my apprenticeship, called my attention to creeds, and set me philosophizing upon them. Perhaps no other circumstance so largely contributed to make me what stupid people call Atheist, and I call Universalist. My intention was to enlarge upon that most important circumstance in this Chapter, but want of space must be my apology for not doing so till the next.

<hr>

CHAPTER IV.

PRIMITIVE DOUBTS.

The Christian who first busied himself about my " spiritual welfare" was the cause of my primitive doubts respecting religious systems. With best intentions he produced worst results. This innocent criminal was a Finisher in the firm of Broadwood and Sons, where I believe he is still employed, and still respected as a conscientiously religious and upright man. No one questioned his honesty though many had strange misgivings as to his intellect, which, truth to tell, was not of the brightest kind. Fond of talking about religion he was frequently engaged in discussions with fellow workmen of the incredulous school, who, carrying too many guns for poor "James," battered him unmercifully. I felt peculiarly strong regard for him, and day after day stood by his bench and attentively listened to his pious exhortations. Unluckily he did not stop with the attempt to *talk* me into his way of thinking, but urged me to *read* several of his books. One of them was a volume of Sermons by the celebrated Timothy Dwight, whose masterly and pious eloquence has long been the theme of christian tongues. To a single passage of that remarkable book I owe my first sceptical thought concerning the superstitious systems priests and their abettors have the impudence to call pure Christianity. After enlarging upon the magnificence of Nature, and the power of Deity as manifested in its creation and preservation, he exclaims with startling earnestness:— *How vain then must be all resistance to God! But the very power, the will, the wish to resist cannot rise into being unless supplied and supported by Him."*

On coming to these words, so deeply significant, I paused and in terrified astonishment literally gasped for breath. The shock was so great that for a time reason seemed to have abandoned her seat, leaving me a prey to conflicting and most painful emotions. "What," thought I, after recovering my presence of mind, "is it indeed true that the power, the will, the wish to resist God is supplied and supported by himself. And can it be true that he will eternally punish for a resistance himself has caused ? Reason at once rejected the monstrous supposition, but with fear and trembling, I went to my Mentor in the hope that he would put in a truthful light what appeared to me so outrageously blasphemous. But vain hope! he could only make visible the darkness in which my soul was plunged. He talked to be sure about the incomprehensibility of God—his right to do what he liked without regard to principles we in our ignorance call just—his desire to save sinners through Christ and him crucified, in whom all might believe if so disposed. For an hour, by the shop clock, he enlarged on the efficacy of prayer and Presbyterian chapel going, as a surest cure for that desolating scepticism he shrewdly suspected had taken possession of me. But he wasted breath. As well might Mahommed have expected to talk the mountain out of its place as he to talk me out of my sudden but profound conviction, that a God who caused men to sin could not consistently be angry with or punish them for their sinfulness. Though only twelve years old, and less than half informed upon matters of logic or of faith, my natural sense detected the blasphemous absurdity of a belief which reduced God, in point of wisdom, to a level lower than his grace the-cannot-I-do-what-I-will-with-my-own-Duke of Newcastle. and in point of tyranous cruelty infinitely lower than Henry the Eighth, Caligula, or Nero. Though so young it seemed to me most wickedly blasphemous to assume that divine justice is based upon principles diametrically opposed to human justice, and flying to the incomprensibility of deity as a sort of refuge for destitute logic, appeared a decent way of retreating from the whole question.

Here, then was I, a raw, undiciplined, curious, self-will'd boy, in my frail reasoning bark cast on a shoreless ocean of doubt, without pilot to steer, or star to guide my course. But few people are content to rest in scepticism. Rosseau thought it a state of mind altogether intolerable. He argues that men will rather embrace error than oscillate between contending opinions without choosing any. To a certainty the majority of pious thinkers have an insuperable aversion for scepticism. Unlike that philosopher who considered the road to wisdom was through the portals of doubt, they anathematize doubters as if they were the devil's favorite children. The late Sir Walter Scott, in his Robert of Paris, endeavours to make out a case against doubters, by declaring that *incredulity* not *credulity* has been the prime cause of error, and the crimes to which error gives birth. But such a conclusion belongs to the romance of philosophy and will hardly bear the test of experience as developed in the sober facts of history. They demonstrate that a tendency to blind faith in fictions has been the plague spot and damning curse of our race, and that where incredulity, like Saul, has slain its thousands, credulity, like David, has slain its tens of thousands.

Human nature has rather erred in believing too much than too little. Rather than not believe or pretend to believe enough, an overwhelming majority of us make a merit of believing we believe a host of doctrines altogether incredible because repugnant to natural sense and experience. Men, for example may say they believe and may even believe they believe every one of the Thirty-nine Articles, but that they actually *do* believe in them, only simpletons will allow. We are as apt to impose on ourselves as others, and the credulous mortals who say they believe the Thirty-nine Articles grossly impose upon themselves. How shall any man, even though he have credulity fifty times Christian, believe in a clock with the remarkable capacity of striking less than one? Or what in point of glaring absurdity is fully equal; an immense Being with neither body, nor parts, nor passions—yet every stickler for the Thirty-nine Articles professes to believe this most absurd, incomprehensible, and therefore *unbelievable* proposition, for the second of those articles declares God a being without body, parts, or passions. Up to the period when antagonism to false religion, was fairly aroused within me by the strange, though orthodox, doctrine of Timothy Dwight, I used the term God, as all children do, without attaching to it any definite signification. If it suggested anything it was the figure of a man, with a long gray beard, sitting somewhere in the clouds amidst a crowd of trumpet-blowing human-looking winged messengers, on whose head sat a kingly crown. The god of a child is always very like his father, and my father had he suffered his beard to grow, would " on high " surrounded by angelic beings have " passed muster " as the God of my childish idolatry. Abstract reasonings on the nature of anything are beyond the capacity of mere children, and yet we talk to children about an abstract Being called God, who is without body, parts, or passions. Surely this appears something like giving " to airy nothing a local habitation and a name."

What to think of such a Being would puzzle the cleverest Philadelphia lawyer, and I hope therefore that no good christian will consign me to the bottomless pit, for confessing that until my reasoning powers were shocked into alarming activity by the hideous nakedness of Dr. Dwight's doctrine, all my notions about God were decidedly material, and I am afraid that many children of much larger growth have no wiser ones. Not long since while walking in the splendid Cathedral at Rouen, my attention was drawn to a picture representing Divinity with a shaven crown on a flying visit to a crowd of monks, who stood with open arms ready to graciously receive the creator of heaven and earth. This kind of Deity it must be allowed is very complimentary to monks in obliging them so far as to have his crown shaven, but to any other than Roman Catholic Christians he is represented less spiritually than all respectable deities ought to be. In point of fact *all* Christians worship amplications of themselves, for the simple reason that spirit is not properly an object, and as such can never be worshipped in spirit and in truth. In less than six months after reading James Henderson's imprudently lent book, I made that and many other valuable discoveries. During that six months I usually read seven, sometimes eight hours out of every twenty-four, I panted after knowledge as harts do after waterbrooks. Paley's Evidences and Natural Theology were read with admiration; Laws' Serious Call, and scores of similar works, with disgust. Though unconvinced by Paley's Reasoning, I admired his singular tact and illustrative ability. Perhaps no author has ever equalled Paley in the art of cheating people into acquiescence with false sophistical principles by boldly assuming their truth, and raising upon the assumption arguments so cogent, brilliant, powerful, and full of illustration, that few are not bewitched into forgetfulness of the miserable beggings of questions, and impertinent takings for granted on which they rest. All that is really argument in the famous Natural Theology must be sought for in the three or four first chapters, which important fact I did not discern till a second reading, some ten years after the first. John Locke's Essay on the Human Understanding taught me how to appreciate the wisdom of innate idea—Doctors, and Shaftesbury " Characteristics," helped me to some valuable ideas concerning " things not seen," in which we are admonished to believe at peril of our immortal souls. With respect to both these extraordinary works, and their tendency upon my youthful mind I have something to say hereafter.

CHAPTER V.

YOUTHFUL PECCADILLOES.

THE youth of large towns almost always suffer from a premature and too rapid developement of the sexual instinct. Rosseau demonstrates that important truth in his Emelius—a book no mother should be without. What Buchan is popularly believed to be in physics the Emelius really is in morals. Parents may learn from that most admirable of all educational Treatises how with children time is gained by losing it, and the terrible evils consequent upon a system of education which stimulates mental at the cost of bodily power. Every such system is wholly false and wholly pernicious. To check, not accelerate, the growth of sexualism should be the object of parents. Were that principle acted upon in our treatment of children there would be no occasion to amuse them with fictions about little babies growing in parsley beds or Old Bogie running away with them. So absurdly paradoxical is our system of early training that while inflaming the passions it exhausts the body. By making men of children it makes children of men. What with the lying tales of nurses and lying books of pedants they have little chance to become either strong in mind or sound in body. Perhaps there is no other single vice so exhausting to the body or corrupting to the mind as early indulgence of the sexual instinct. Yet generally speaking the youth of large towns are tempted into, rather than restrained from, such indulgence. In my case continence would have been a miracle. Early thrown upon my own resources which were miserably inadequate, I have ever since been

"Lord of myself that heritage of woe.

During the first years of apprenticeship my wages were insufficient to provide the merest necessaries of life; and fully alive to the necessity of living, and generously too, I did so without much consideration as to consequences. Most of my relatives were either too poor or too selfish to trouble themselves about me, and so for years I was allowed to struggle on amidst a host of constantly increasing difficulties. One of my brothers offered me a home, which, however, I could not bring myself to accept because my love of unrestrained personal liberty was greater than my hatred of gaping creditors. I detested the thought of being *compelled* to go home or to bed at a certain hour. Poor Megrim in the Blue Devils, when soliloquising on the delights of suicide, feelingly descants upon that eternal circle of miseries—getting up, going to breakfast, going to dinner, going to supper, going to bed, and then getting up again.—At thirteen years of age I could sympathise with that unhappy gentleman so far as regarded the dull routine and wretched uniformity of "respectable" families; and never could endure being *forced* to do anything. I already belonged to the class of persons described by Lord Bacon as so fond of liberty that they will not consent to wear waistbands. Convinced that all work and no play makes Jack a dull boy, I deemed it quite logical to conclude it was right to work as little and play as much as possible. I had heard of a happy servant who worked many years without knowing the comfort of a bed, as according to her own account the moment she got into it she fell asleep and got out of it the instant she awoke. A happy life of that kind had no charms for one who like myself detested regularity, had no particular love for hard work, and half-a-dozen times a day was ready to exclaim—anything for a change.

Albert, the son of William Tell, meeting Gesler on the Swiss mountains, that tyrant in the course of conversation with him learning that the stern patriot preferred living there to descending to the plains is curious to know *why*, asking the boy what his father would lose by doing so. *His liberty*—was the short but pithy reply. And liberty was just what I feared to lose by taking up my abode with such relatives as might have been willing but certainly were not eager to receive me. The notion crept into my head that though good living, shelter, and clothing are excellent things, we may pay too dearly for them. I therefore preferred hard fare with much (far too much) liberty to " the Sauces of Dives" altogether without it. And even now though much improved in this particular I hate any other restraint than what is imposed by my own reason; and perhaps no man on earth better appreciates that beautiful passage in Sterne—*Oh, Slavery disguise thee as thou wilt; still thou art a bitter draught, and though thousands in all ages have been made to taste thee thou art none the less bitter on that account.*

With so insane a love of liberty no one can be surprised to learn that I often pushed it to licentiousness and upon the principle of a short life and a merry one, made sad mistakes. Not that my life *was* a merry one; far from it. Poets tell us the season of youth is the season of pleasure; but I found it a season of misery. Plunged in debt and tormented by desires neither to be satisfied nor repressed, my way of life was full of thorns. My greatest danger arose from that precocious development of the instinct already referred to. Alone in the world, without parents to control or friends to advise me, I went rapidly down the broad path which leadeth to destruction. When Epictetus was asked why Venus was painted naked, he said—*Because she leaves her worshippers without a rag to cover them.* My adoration at her shrine more than once reduced me to that primitive but unpleasant condition; and many a pound have I borrowed to relieve myself from the state, which though called *puris naturalibus* I thought anything but agreeable to nature. It is not recorded how many sweethearts *young* Soloman had, but we have it on Scriptural authority that *old* Solomon of wives and concubines could boast a stock of one thousand or thereabouts. Judging from what he did when old we may infer that he was a devil of a fellow when young. I would willingly prove as much because my opinion decidedly is that extreme love of woman is no proof of extreme corruption in man. On the contrary I believe that generally speaking they are the best men who have the most regard for the other sex, and though I do not deem it safe for woman to put firm faith in the proverb *that reformed rakes make the best husbands,* I am sure it is frequently found to be the case. Pharisees may object but it is none the less true that careful, because *cold-blooded,* youths seldom develope into noble hearted or clear headed men. I would not be understood to justify, or even apologise for vice of any kind—nothing can be more remote from my intention. I deplore the premature development and misdirection of the sexual instinct, consequent upon a system of training we miscall education. Were I a father, to preserve my son from too early and irregular intercourse with the other sex would be my chief care, and my opinion is that every father ought to raise his voice against that most wretched of all mock morality which hinders gevernment from taking houses of ill fame under its special surveillance. *Pas trop governe* is a maxim I do not dispute the wisdom of; but statesmen, while careful to avoid governing too much, should avoid the error of governing too little. In France, arrangements with regard to irregular intercourse of the sexes, though far from perfect, are greatly in advance of those established in our own country. In France, courtezans are watched controlled and protected by the State. With us, they are neither watched nor controlled nor protected. All is *hap-hazard* with respect to them, and will so remain until the pharisaical spirit shall die the death decreed for it by the spirit of wisdom. In this pious country the practice is to strain at gnats and swallow camels, the most abominable evils being covertly encouraged by the State if they serve some political or party purpose—a fact signally illustrated in the different treatment received by different classes of courtezans. Well might the poet say—

> *Vice* is undone, if she forgets her birth,
> And stoops from angels to the dregs of earth;
> But 'tis the *fall* degrades her to the whore;
> Let greatness own her and she's mean no more.
> Her birth, her beauty, crowds and courts confess,
> Chaste matrons praise her, and grave bishops bless;
> In golden chains the willing world she draws,
> And hers the gospel is, and hers the laws;
> Mounts the tribunal, lifts her scarlet head,
> And sees pale virtue carted in her stead.

Oh! CANT what crimes are committed by thy adorers. How impudently dost thou usurp the throne of Honesty. But Reason will dethrone the tyrant. Yes, that Reason so much vilified, *because so much dreaded*, by corrupt and foolish men, will sooner or later separate the wheat from the chaff of human morality, and gathering the wheat into garners will burn up the chaff with unquenchable fire. Then that sexual instinct whose perversion we deplore will in all cases be made conducive to the best interests of states instead of being, as it now is, a prime cause of their corruption and overthrow.

CHAPTER VI.

FIRST LOVE.

Go tell love it is but lust, is a sentiment ascribed to Sir Walter Raleigh, and one with which I cannot agree. Experience has convinced me that lust is not the only feeling which operates on men in their sexual association with the softer sex. After a five years' career of alternate virtue and vice, profligacy, and earnest searching after the good, useful, and true, I fell in love with a girl about my own age, of humble but respectable parents. No love could be sincerer or more devoted than mine: to kiss the very ground on which she trod was deemed a happiness, and the tying up her shoe-string, or even touching the hem of her garment, sufficed to fill my soul with most exquisite sensations.

> She was a form of life and light,
> Which seen became a part of sight,
> And rose where'er I turned my eye,
> The morning star of memory.

How this was I cannot say, but that so it was I know. Without doubt, beauty is rested in the lover's fancy, and to my fancy Mary Seaford appeared the most beautiful of all beautiful beings; yet neither face nor form would bear a critical examination. Her figure was sylph-like, but considerably below the middle size; while her face, though wonderfully expressive, was inferior in point of outline and regularity of feature. She had that kind of beauty which is murdered by dissection; though

> Her eyes' dark charm 'twere vain to tell,
> But gaze on that of the gazelle,
> It will assist thy fancy well;
> As large, as languishingly dark,
> But soul beam'd forth in every spark
> That darted from beneath the lid,
> Bright as the jewel of Giamschid.

In no other way can I account—so satisfactorily account—for my singularly passionate admiration of this girl, as by reference to those expressive and fascinating eyes, by the ever active fires of which my poor heart was well nigh reduced to cinders. I am a great

admirer of ladies' eyes, and profess to be a tolerably
good judge, having seen the glorious black ones of
Spain, France, and many other countries, but never
have I met with a pair so bewitching as hers.   This is
not a lover's rhapsody, which the reader will be assured of when I say that she I first loved, though
afterwards my wife, forfeited all title to my love, and
assuredly lost it long before her death.   What caused
so great a revolution in my youthful feelings towards
one for whom I had felt such devoted affection, will
appear from the following brief but faithful recital of
events :—

At a very early age I had manifested a strong desire
to strut and fret my hour upon the dramatic stage.
When a mere infant I received immense applause for
reciting (as they told me) with due emphasis and good
discretion, " My Name is Norval," "Now stood Eliza
on the Wood-crowned Height," and other school-boy
pieces.   My eccentric old Irish nurse, poor Molly
Croker (who insisted upon it that her nurslings were
the cleverest of created beings), made' me believe myself a Roscius in petticoats, and almost as soon as I was
breeched, I united with other young Rosciuses to get
up private plays, in which I greatly distinguished
myself.   All the world prophecied I should in time
become a good actor, which prophecy has unfortunately
not been justified by events.   It is probable, indeed,
that I might have become a good stage-player if my
inclinations had steadily pointed that way.   It was
while strutting about in sock and buskin that I first
met the first goddess of my idolatry.   She and her
parents were charmed by my performance of Lord
Randolph in Homes' tragedy of Douglas, and shortly
after I was invited to their house, where my rattling
talk and wonderful flow of animal spirits made me a
very welcome guest.   There it was, as Count de Val-
mont says, I welcomed love, but cannot add with him,
a first, a last, an only and eternal passion; for, as
already intimated, my first love has not been my last,
nor indeed the strongest I have felt for one of the other
sex.   My love seemed to be, and I believe really was,
returned.   Of her many lovers the charming Mary
selected me, although I was miserably jealous, often
extremely insolent under the green-eyed monster's influence, and naturally of an overbearing disposition.
But there were some peculiarities of character dis-

played by me during courtship which I feel much satisfaction in reflecting upon, and do most heartily desire that lovers in general would exhibit them more markedly than they are wont to do. One of these I will enlarge upon, for the two-fold purpose of stimulating courting readers to imitation, and laying bare what I consider an honorable, but others may think a ridiculous weakness.

Such was my fear of being chosen as a husband, and afterwards not loved better than my less fortunate rivals, that whenever I knew they were at the house, I studiously absented myself from it. For weeks I would not see her on whom my soul doated; and when, by accident or appointment, we met at some party of friends, and she (which was always the case) reproached me for my strange neglect, my reply was, "Mary, I love you devotedly, sincerely, and because I do so love, cannot bear the thought of seeming to force your inclinations, which might be the case did I press my suit in presence of a host of rivals. I, under such circumstances, leave you free to act in harmony with those sincere feelings which I never will willingly outrage; and if your love for me is one thousandth part as strong and pure as mine for you, absence will neither destroy nor weaken it." To that she assented, but still with many tears assured me she could not bear my absence. I believed her, little dreaming what anguish and bitter disappointment Providence had in store for me. Affairs of an important nature, coupled with the desire of her parents to get a better match for their daughter than I was likely to prove, separated us for about two years, when our intimacy was renewed, and we were married. From her conduct towards me I judged that she was faithful and loving as ever; but, alas! frailty, thy name is woman. In less than a week after our marriage, I discovered what left me little room to doubt the infidelity of my wife. Some eccentricities of conduct had not passed unnoticed by me; but up to the day on which we parted, the suspicion that she was a jilt never crossed my mind. On that day my proud feelings were put to the severest of all trials, and triumphantly did they pass the worse than fiery ordeal.

Old Orpheus knew a good wife's worth so well,
That when his died he followed her to hell;
And for her loss, at the Elysian grove,
He did not only ghosts to pity move,
But the sad poet breath'd his sighs so deep,
'Tis said the devils could not choose but weep.

But the love for Eurydice here ascribed to Orpheus did not—could not exceed that deep and strong affection I then felt for Mary Seaford. In the world I loved none but her, and on separating from her, as I thought, for ever, could with perfect sincerity have exclaimed with Othello—"If heaven would make me such another world of one entire and perfect chrysolite, I'd not have sold her for it." Nevertheless, with icy coldness I listened to the tale which convinced me she was an adultress in heart if not in fact.

I had long resided in the house where that distressing scene took place, it is my intention to describe. It had been my abiding place for years before marriage. The landlady was a kind-hearted woman, and I believe entertained for me sincere respect and motherly affection She it was who discovered and made known what would not have been credited but for corroborative evidence altogether indisputable because admitted to be true by the fair deceiver herself. Its sum was this. During our two years separation her youthful fancy had been captivated by a young man named Horace Partington, who had that alluring look, 'twixt man and woman, which I have found to charm the more fantastic dames. But he either did not wish, or found it inconvenient to marry, and so the lady honored me by becoming my wife, no doubt consoling herself with the reflection that if marriage served no other useful pnrpose, at least it served for a blind. When the damning tale was told which convinced me she was foul as Vulcan's stithy; when in her own presence it was proved that even on our wedding day, during my temporary absence on matters of import, she had stolen to her lover; when I silently stood, my heart wrung with anguish, mentally cursing the hour in which I first saw the light, she unabashed, and with strumpet-like audacity said— "Well, it is all true; and another truth is, I only married you as a convenience." My reply was a look of unutterable contempt; and though my lips quivered, with the *sang froid* of a veteran gamester I turned towards the horrified landlady, and said—" Madam, your kindness will never be forgotten by me, but the state of my affairs compels me to leave your hospitable roof. As for this young lady, she may stay here, or if *convenience* so prescribe, go elsewhere; with me she shall *not* remain—from this moment we part for ever." Without caring to observe the effect of these words, I shook my old landlady's hand, and coolly putting on my hat, as coolly left the house.

CHAPTER VII.

FIRST PERJURY

WHOM *God hath joined together let no man put asunder,* is a good commandment; but what should be done with those unfortunate couples whom the Devil hath joined together. Unhappy marriages are not like angels visits; indeed, there are so many of them, that whether the rule or the exception is a point difficult of determination; and saying they were *made in heaven* is a poor reply to those who would have them unmade on earth. Undoubtedly our law recognises divorce but after a fashion so strange as to justify the wit who likened it to the spider's web, which, though strong enough to catch small flies, can't hold bluebottles. Divorce is allowed to those who are rich enough to pay for it, with the proviso that the parties seeking a divorce render themselves worthy of so signal a favor by the commission of adultery. Poor people are not allowed such luxuries. They may form ill assorted unions—marry in haste and repent at leisure; but, being poor, the law says you shall not separate; no, not even though you open the way for so blest a consummation by committing adultery. Get rich, commit, or *seem* to commit adultery, and divorce shall be your reward. This is the language of law—the law of England—that *human reason in perfection,* of which, judges tell us, Christianity is part and parcel. When Lady Ellenborough made a cuckold of her liege lord, he carried his case to the House of Peers, and divorce was pronounced. My wife was false; she confessed it, gloried in it; but not being a bluebottle, I could not break through the web our legal spiders have so well contrived for the catching of small flies. What,

then, was I to do? Not twenty years of age, with
heart cruelly lacerated and brain on fire, the law
afforded no redress, no consolation. To be sure, it
was open to me. Oh yes, I could have sued for a
divorce in our Hospital of Incurables upon the same
principle (to borrow the happy idea of Sheridan) that
the half famished, penniless beggar can enter the
London tavern and sue for a good dinner. What then
was I to do? The answer of philosophy is—be resigned. Well, I *tried* to be so. For many months,
with " the winged shaft deep in my heart," I labored
to regain that peace of mind which truly doth pass
all understanding; and remembering a passage by
Doctor Johnson, to the effect that we can best destroy
one passion by the excitement of another, I applied
myself to study with frenzied earnestness. Books
were my greatest, my only consolation; and paradoxical though it may seem, many a time, with hot tears
streaming down my cheeks, have I exclaimed with
Fenelon, " Happy, thrice happy, are those who love
to read." At that period I prosecuted the study of
French, and so successfully, that in three months I
could read French books, and write what competent
judges have pronounced tolerably good French love
letters. As a proof of the perseverance with which
I pursued this kind of study, I may mention that in
foolish compliance with the advice of poor old Cobbett, I wrote twice over in a little book, which was
my constant companion, every noun in Boyer's French
Dictionary. To the account of excessive application
to every kind and order of books may be laid that
nervous irritability which distinguishes me. It is
worthy of observation that I am commonly most nervous when there is least cause for fear. I, who have
stood in the battle-field amid a shower of bullets,
without moving a muscle, or allowing my serenity to
be the least disturbed—I, who for ten hours, before a
besotted judge, and still more besotted jury, pleaded
my own cause in the city of Bristol, without " bating
one jot of heart or hope"—I, who have been stoned
and hooted by infuriate mobs, without caring whether
the bigotted beasts tore me to pieces or not—have felt,
as it were, my heart leap into my mouth at the name
of a friend, and trembled from head to foot at sight
of a letter. Often have I stood at the door of a house

from whose inmates was expected nothing but welcome, with the knocker in my hand, hesitating to let it fall lest I should be unable to calmly address those who opened it. Some one relates that Bailley, the eminent revolutionist, on his march to the scaffold trembled violently, which a gen d'arme observing, said, " You shake, Sir." " It is with cold, then," was the quick reply. And that Bailley was no coward his death as well as life amply testifies.

> The flesh will quiver where the pincers tear,
> The blood will follow where the knife is driven,
> But these are foreign to the soul.

It is a mistake to suppose that quivering flesh is sufficient evidence of mental cowardice or that nervousness is always indicative of unfitness to play the boldest part. No reformer of modern times has played a *bolder* part than myself. That fact being patent to all the world, no one is entitled to accuse me of Bobadilism for confessing it, and yet the merest trifles of every day life, such as the wanted shirt wanting a shirt button, or "cut direct" from some coquettish lady who promised to be my partner in the dance, has often begot in me a tremulousness and a fluster of spirits altogether unaccountable. My belief is that excessive anxiety for the loss of my wife combined with that excessive studiousness to which I resorted to kill thought and thus deaden the severity of affliction, were the seeds of this mischief, which I am happy to say is becoming less and less potent with me. It is to be feared that the sword of my spirit will always be too sharp for its scabbard, but a constant habit of blunting the edge of it may do much.

About four months after separating from my hopeful wife, I was visited by her Aunt—a fascinating woman of thirty-two. She came to advise and condole with me on the disastrous state of my affairs. I was young, she was not old and assuredly one of the most lively and agreeable women I ever beheld. She was an unmarried mother who, when a mere girl, had been seduced and abandoned by one of the many villains who will gratify their lust—no matter at what expense to their unsuspecting victims. From the period when that misfortune befell her up to the time of her visit to me, even scandal allowed that she had led an irreproachable life. Like ladies'-maids in general, she

was the picture of neatness, and withal there was
something about her so *piquant*, and taking, that wiser
youths than myself might have been excused for falling in love with her.   There are countenances, *female*
countenances too, which on beholding specimens of,
I am tempted to say, as Octavian does after examining
the face of old Roque—*Providence has slubbered it in
haste, it is one of her unmeaning compositions she manu-
factures when she makes a gross.   She will form a million
such and all alike, then send them forth ashamed of her
work, and set no mark upon them.*   But the countenance
of my fair friend, to whom the reader has just been
introduced, was' neither slobbered in haste, nor an
unmeaning composition, and assuredly Providence had
no sufficient cause to be ashamed of her.   Not only
had she a good-natured charming face, but a figure
admirably proportioned, and slightly above the middle height.   Of her feet and legs (always exhibited to
the best advantage) I dare not trust myself to say
more than that they would have suffered little by
comparison with the "model" ones of Madame Vestris.
Add to all these brain bewildering attractions, a
graceful and easy carriage, you have my dangerous
visitor as she appeared to me, with the serious draw-
back of not being able to feel, as I did, the influence
of her matchless smile which disclosed between lips
that "shamed the rose's hue" two rows of even, pearly
teeth·

Her first visit was speedily followed by a second,
until the pleasure of meeting became so great, that
for many weeks not a day elapsed without my heart
being warmed and cheered by the presence of this new
flame.   But though delighted with her society, the
idea of popping any improper question either never
occurred to me, or was dismissed the moment it entered my head, until one day she astonished me by a
gentle, but unmistakeable hint that regard for character would preclude her from coming any more to my
lodgings or indeed being on intimate terms with me
anywhere unless I would promise to marry her.   This
for a man already blessed with one wife was a home
thrust.   But though not over scrupulous about marriage vows, which my wife had been the first to break,
I had insuperable objections to being tried for bigamy.
The bare possibility of such a thing was enough to
scare me from all indulgence of libidinous desire.

Historians affirm that so great were the fascinations of Cleopatra, the beautiful Queen of Egypt, that for the joy of passing a night with her many men were willing to pay the penalty of death in the morning. But as Byron says—

The cold in clime are cold in blood

And I was cold-blooded enough to refuse the life-long companionship of a delightful woman, at the trifling cost of possible trial for bigamy. In vain my fair friend protested that she would rather die than betray me. The *possibility* of so unpoetic a termination to our amour, and my natural distaste for a second marriage, after making so terrible a mistake in the first, rendered all such protestations unavailing. Finding me obdurate, the lady softened apace, but ever and anon assured me she never would be mine except by way of marriage. In Platonic style we continued to act towards each other, till one fine but unlucky evening when Cupid was more than a match for Plato, my charming friend, divorced from all discretion, like Donna Inez under similar circumstances,

Whispering she would ne'er consent—consented,

and I was betrayed into the commission of my FIRST PERJURY.

CHAPTER VIII.

MORE MISHAPS.

BARON SWEDENBORG, in his almost forgotten book on " Scortatory Love," assigns to the act of keeping a mistress the delicate and scientific name of Pellicacy. But however scientific or delicate may be the name of a bad thing it is none the less bad.

Not all that heralds rake from coffin'd clay,
Nor florid prose, nor honied lies of rhyme,
Can blazon evil deeds or consecrate a crime.

There is, nevertheless, much—very much in a name. Pellicacy, for example, reads better than Fornication, though its meaning be the same, and will do so to the end of the chapter. We honor the poet who said the rose by any other name would smell as sweet;

but, in rigid adherence to my conviction that he who sets about confessing sundry high crimes and misdemeanors should carefully select the most delicate terms, I choose Pellicacy to describe my act of living with the dangerous visitor referred to in my last. As man and wife we were together for six months or thereabouts, when, much to my annoyance, our felicity was disturbed by the news that my legal *cara sposa*, devoured by remorse and jealousy, was fast journeying towards that mysterious bourne whence no traveller returns. She had evidently made the double mistake of misjudging her own strength and my weakness—a mistake often made by young married women who are blest or curst with blind-as-bats, adoring husbands. When too late she discovered her error. The studied coldness with which I parted from her and bitterly ironical style of my expressions had stung her to the heart. Fully sensible of her own attractions she did not dream that the spell which bound me to her could be so suddenly dissolved. My conduct had astonished, humiliated her; and when we again lived together, which we did shortly after, she often said that immediately on separating her early affection for me revived with ten-fold force; and in such cases absence frequently does " make the heart grow fonder" than it ever could be while present with its object.

Distance lends enchantment to the view.

And I am firm in the faith that many, if not all married couples would find occasional separation a mighty provocative of love. Bulwer hints as much in one of his novels, where we are introduced to a three or four months married couple, who, without themselves being sensible of the fact, find disgust gradually usurping the place of affection. I almost forget how the tale runs, but, to the best of my recollection, all at once the lady discovers that her husband has a cast in his eye, which she fears may be mistaken for a squint, and as suddenly the husband detects not a beauty but a blemish spot on the fair cheek of his wife. The physician called in understands precisely the nature of the case, and as a remedy for it prescribes a short journey for the happy couple upon the separate principle. They set out in different directions, return and meet in the course of a few weeks, forgot all about the blemishes she had before been so quick to detect; and on her return to me (about which I shall iu due time speak more at large) was far more affectionate than I then wished her to be. But what "like a poisonous mineral gnawed her inwards" was my connection with the aunt. It aroused within her a feeling of jealousy, all the more poignant and desolating because coupled with remorse. Under the influence of those terrible feelings she became grievous sick and took to her bed where for weeks she remained in a state truly pitiable. Medical men were called in but soon found physic did not reach the seat of her disease, and might just as well have been thrown to the dogs.

> Canst thou not minister to a mind diseas'd;
> Pluck from the memory a rooted sorrow;
> Raze out the written troubles of the brain;
> And, with some sweet oblivious antidote,
> Cleanse the foul bosom of that perilous stuff
> Which weighs upon the heart?

Macbeth, who puts this question, is thus answered by the physician :—

> Therein the patient must minister to himself.

Many diseases are beyond the reach of medicine, and these chiefly are what we expressively call diseases of the heart. They who acutely suffer from them must. indeed, minister to themselves.

Now, let others judge of me harshly as they will, I *know* myself humane. When I read in books or newspapers of wretches who, actuated by a spirit of wanton, deliberate cruelty, torture that noble animal the horse, or that patient, useful, but ill-used animal, the ass, all the blood of my body seems to rush impetuously towards my head, and reason is lost in indignation. Were I dictator, the savage who tormented animals should be dealt with after a fashion that would surprise this canting generation. For dogs I have so strong an affection that people laugh at the anxiety I manifest with regard to their comfort and general welfare. I do not now keep any, because when I did the fear of their getting kicked, half-starved, or otherwise ill used, cost me many anxious hours. In Scotland I had two, one called Punch and the other Judy.   Notwithstanding my great care they both died.   Like a coquette deprived of her lovers, I was inconsolable for their loss.   If cruel at all, it is only to animals of my own species; and tender-hearted readers will, perhaps, think I was far from humane when, on learning the conscience stricken and dangerous state of my wife, I manifested no inclination either to console or see her.   Well-meaning relatives pressed me to forgive and forget; but though able to forgive I knew not how to forget.   She had played me false, and to that (as we custom-moulded people think) deepest of all injuries had added insult.   *I only married you for convenience* were words not to be forgotten.   It is easy for people to moralize upon such subjects, and gravely or glibly talk about what they would or would not do if placed in similar circumstances, but only self can adequately judge for self. We are told

> God was the first that marriage did ordain
> By making one two and two one again.

and I care not to dispute the fact; but it happened that though my lawful wife and myself were made "one, two," I had not the slightest inclination any time after her avowal of infidelity to be made "two one" again.   Besides, my experience of Pellicacy had shown that keeping a *good* mistress was more productive of happiness than keeping a *bad* wife.   And who, after all, are prostitutes?   Not those, assuredly, who are held together by the strong tie of affection but those who own no other than a legal bond.   Every one admits connection without affection to be prostitution, and yet thousands unblushingly drag their slow length of life along with partners whom they loathe. These are veritable prostitutes.   Against the institution of marriage I have nothing to say; but where the priest joins "hands, not hearts," what but prostitution can result?   Consecrated and legalized crime may appear respectable in the eye of folly, but wise men know how to appreciate it.   The woman with whom I lived was faithful; the woman I married was false. In the former I found a kind, generous, and loving companion; in the latter an ignorant, selfish, and most impudent jilt.   Tell me, ye wise saints who preach up the morality of legalized prostitution, which of these two women best deserved all the kindness and consideration in my power to bestow? All save yourselves will, as I did, declare at once for the most worthy. But, alas!

> Men are the sport of circumstances, when
> Circumstances seem the sport of men.

My wife's relatives allowed me neither rest nor peace till I had seen her. I was shocked and softened by the sight. She was the merest phantom of her former self. Grief had humiliated her spirit, and that fell disease of the heart no physic can cure had eaten away the flesh from her bones, and given to her complexion a deathlike hue while imparting to her sunken eyes an expression of unceasing anguish and supernatural brilliancy. To dwell upon this picture would be painful to me; I therefore dismiss it with the single remark, that my resolution never again to live with her as a husband deserted me the moment I entered the room. Philosophy gone, passion took its place; and both her trembling hands in mine, I essayed to comfort her; but feelings too strong for utterance were at work within me and, burying my face in her pillow, I burst into tears.

CHAPTER IX.

POLITICAL DEBUT.

THERE is a more intimate connection between free-thinking in religion and freethinking in politics than is commonly supposed. They who reason themselves into contempt for the jargon of priests are far more likely than those who do not to penetrate the designs and see through the humbug of statesmen. A habit of taking opinions upon trust is inimical to a just appreciation of words or things. Political imposters in high places are so well aware of this, that they move heaven and earth against any popular tendency to *examine* opinions before *subscribing* to them. They treat the governed as cunning schoolboys treat credulous little fellows who open their mouths and shut their eyes just to see what God will send them. Our political, like our religious system, won't bear discus-

sion. "Take the sceptre, break it; it is the king.
Take the cross, break it; it is the priest·" No wonder then that monarchs and priests should commonly
affect for each other what they do not feel, or fight side
by side against their common enemy—discussion.
Into each others hands they play the game of politics,
and all know with what result. Kingcraft and priest-
craft, like the famous twins of Siam, cannot afford to
" cut the connection." They are two in name, one in
essence ; and reformers who think priests *as such* can
bear rule among a free people, or monarchs reign without priests, are miserably deceived. I was early convinced of this. No sooner did I reason myself into
contempt of organized religion than I began to suspect
"there must be something wrong " in our system of
government. The scales fallen from my eyes, I did
not see men as trees walking, but men as fools acting.
Having shuffled off all respect for big words about big
nothings, all insane idolatry for unreal entities, my
respect for statesmen who govern through belief in
them soon gave up the ghost. But not until after the
events recorded in former chapters did I take an active part in politics. Having consented again to live
with my wife, I felt more than ever disgusted with my
circumstances. As might have been foretold, she did
not please me as at first. When affairs going wrong
embarrassments increasing, and conscience disturbed
by the reflection that her aunt had been unjustly and
cruelly abandoned, I got quite " out at elbows " with
the world, and could truly say with the murderer in
Macbeth—

> So weary with disasters, tugged with fortune,
> That I would set my life on any chance
> To mend it or be rid of it.

To mend or be rid of my life I was resolved, and in
hope of *mending* it began business as a bookseller. The
times were "out of joint;" political questions were
eagerly discussed. Judge Williams, by his cruel
treatment of the Dorchester labourers, fanned the
flame of popular discontent. The Trades Unionists
were never before so powerful or so resolved upon some
great organic change in our "glorious constitution.'
The star of Whiggery began to " pale its ineffectua
fire," and coming events cast shadows before of a cha

racter portentous and gloomy. Old political parties
began to live by eating their own heads off; and that
class emphatically called the working class, whom the
Bishop of Manchester delighteth to honor with the
distinctive appellation of MOST respectable, had serious
misgivings or rather suspicions as to the near approach
of " a good time coming," when they must live by
eating each other. From the Land's End to John
O'Groat's house was one vast hot bed of sedition.
Liberty and justice, outraged in the persons of the poor
laborers of Dorsetshire, were avenged by Trades
Unionists, who, more than sixteen thousand strong,
marched from White Conduit House to the Home
Office to petition ministers. A glorious sight was that
procession, so calm, so orderly, so full of meaning—a
meaning well understood by the then ministers, who
dared neither generously grant nor absolutely deny its
prayer. Lord Grey, though pledged to " stand by his
order," felt the expediency of temporizing—a policy in
which Whigs are adepts. Their Reform Bill had been
weighed in the balance and found wanting. Reformers
of all shades subscribed to the new faith that they had
got the bill, the whole bill, and *nothing but* the bill.
Political and trades unions hard at work, ministers
alarmed—Toryism, a dumb dog, because afraid to bark
everything disturbed, nothing settled, and agitation
the order of the day—I prepared myself for a plunge
into the troubled ocean of politics. After our reunion
my wife's health rapidly improved, and with some
difficulty I opened a shop near Stretton Ground,
Westminster, chiefly for the sale of Pioneers, Moral
Worlds, and other periodicals of an ultra-liberal stamp.
I succeeded beyond all anticipation; but when I
thought " full sure my greatness was a ripening,"
there came " a frost—a killing frost;" for my wife·
again fell sick, and therefore unable to manage business of any kind. Her two orphan sisters, whom at
her request I had permitted to reside with us, added
to my embarrassments. Suddenly deprived of both
their parents, I could not very well refuse to give them
such food and shelter as my limited means would
permit. But bitterly did I regret having anything to
do with them; for more thankless, useless, idle bag-
gages no man ever yet hampered himself with. The
sufferings I then endured will never be forgotten

"while memory holds her seat in this distracted globe," and will at least have the one good effect of making me think twice before giving way to the impulses of humanity in favor of people who can please nothing but relationship as title to consideration. The two with whom I was plagued were fit for nothing, if we except ministering to their own vanity, and obeying to the very letter that boarding-school injunction that young ladies should always sit prim, look pale, and eat peas and pudding with a fork. With a wife so ill as to be unable to assist me in any one particular, and the two nice young ladies, her sisters, it will readily be understood that my business melted away with the agitation which may be said to have given it birth. After vainly struggling against the tide of adversity, I closed the shop, and went into private lodgings. But my political tendencies were no less marked, and my political aspirations more ambitious than ever. I soon joined a number of liberal politicians in taking a room where radical lectures should be delivered, and education, free from the taint of sectarianism, be given to the children in our locality. We succeeded in obtaining a building in Westminster tolerably well suited to our purpose, to which we gave the rather presumptuous name of Rational School. There it was I made my political debut. I had, to be sure, often taken a part in the proceedings of debating societies, and been accounted a promising speaker prior to the establishment of that school. But there it was I first took part in public proceedings in a public capacity. The occasion was favorable to the display of such talking power as I then possessed, and I had the satisfaction of hearing on all sides that my political debut was, as Osrick says, " a hit, a hit, a palpable hit." The meeting was called to protest against certain proceedings taken by the clergy against the venders of " blasphemous " publications. On rising to speak I felt considerable trepidation, but warming with my subject, I poured out a flood of words which astonished none so much as myself. The patent receipt for writing a good love-letter is to begin without knowing what you are going to say, and to end without knowing what you have said. I made my maiden speech upon exactly that principle. What I was going to say God may have known, but assuredly I did not, and at the conclusion I should have been sorely puzzled to remember what I had been talking about. Perhaps, however, it was none the worse on that account. *Impromptu* speeches, *faites a loiser*, are not always the best; and after ten years experience as a public lecturer and public debater, my conviction is, that the most effective and truly eloquent speeches are made by those who begin without knowing what they are going to say, and end without knowing what they have said. The finest speeches ever delivered by the famous Mirabeau, were, according to his own admission, those he had taken the least pains to "cook up" materials for. His plan was to know something about the subject in hand, and trust for guidance while treating it to the immediate impulses of his own vast genius. Few can imitate him with the least chance of success. My own oratorical powers I esteem but lightly. Always able to make *a* speech, I am rarely able to make *the* speech. But by far the most effective and in every sense of the word, best speeches I ever made, were made on the spur of the moment, without preparation or five minutes previous deliberation. From the first I was thought to distinguish myself rather as a ready than a logical talker, one who found it far easier to amuse and astonish than to instruct or convince. Being a modest man I presume not to give judgment in this matter, leaving so difficult and delicate a task to others better entitled to offer an opinion.

CONFESSIONS OF A FREETHINKER.

CHAPTER X.

NARROW ESCAPE.

THE political debut was speedily followed by the death of my wife, who yielded up her breath after a tedious and distressing illness. Throughout that illness she manifested a spirit truly heroic, often for hours together talking with perfect calmness about her approaching decease. She seemed, indeed, more anxious about what would happen to me when she was gone, than her own manner of going, or the "infinite obscure" towards which she felt herself irresistibly impelled. That world unknown beyond the grave, on which even Addison confessed,

" Darkness, clouds, and shadows rest,"

had no hold upon her imagination. Like all from whom hope is not entirely shut out, she would fain have clung to life, but happily was superior to the vain fear of that nothing called death, which moral monsters and their superstitious slaves dress up as grisly despot and king of terrors. Without the philosophy she had the philosophic tendencies of Jeremy Bentham. During her last three weeks of life she occupied herself almost exclusively in making such arrangements for the future as would entail the least inconvenience upon her friends and relatives. All regard for self seemed absorbed and lost in regard for others. Strange as to some it may appear, she did not desire to be buried, but earnestly enjoined me to have her body dissected, and the articulated bones carefully preserved in some college of surgeons. She considered dissection of the dead most useful to the living, and smiled at popular horror concerning it. Moreover, there was in her, as in myself, a rooted aversion to being " decently interred in a churchyard, with stinking rogues who rot in winding sheets—the common dung of the soil."

Were freethinking the rule not the exception among us, the popular prejudice against a rational mode of dealing with the dead would cease to exist. On this, as on every other important subject, the people are hoodwinked by a clergy, nine in ten of whom in some way or other have a vested interest in stinks, and thrive by the corruption of our graveyards. None but a grossly superstitious and therefore priestridden people, would tolerate the existence of burial grounds in the heart of our towns and cities. A wise population would take care that the air we breathe should not be loaded with poisonous miasma, in order to enrich a far too rich and ever grasping priesthood. Whatever tends to diminish our insane dread of death will infallibly diminish priestly and add to popular power. The poet of all ages, immortal Shakspeare, has bequeathed us a wise lesson on this subject in his Measure for Measure, where the Duke says to Claudio—

Be absolute for death; either death or life
Shall thereby be the sweeter.   Reason thus with life—
If I do lose thee, I do lose a thing
That none but fools would keep: a breath thou art,
(Servile to all the skyey influences,)
That dost this habitation, where thou keep'st
Hourly afflict: merely thou art death's fool;
For him thou labour'st by thy flight to shun,
And yet run'st toward him still.   Thou art not noble;
For all the accommodations that thou bear'st
Are nursed by baseness.   Thou art by no means valiant;
For thou dost fear the soft and tender fork
Of a poor worm.   Thy best of rest is sleep,
And that thou oft provok'st; yet grossly fear'st
Thy death, which is no more.

The lugubrious parapharnalia of funerals, which
is the stock in trade of sacerdotal imposters, will
rank among the absurdities that were, when the
mind of our country, now vulgarized by error, shall
by refined and purified by rational education.   The
convenient scarecrow priests call conscience will cease
to be *scared* by a death's head with a bone in the
mouth, or take offence at any arrangement with regard
to the dead which shall contribute to the health and
morality of the living.   In these sentiments my wife
shared.   She neither dreaded death as something too
terrible for mortal thought to occupy itself upon, nor
felt the least inclination to become food for worms in
an orthodox grave, whose pestilential exhalations
would spread disease around.

Perhaps in both of us this rooted aversion to the
ordinary mode of interment was closely connected
with a prudent horror of being buried alive.   Notwithstanding what certain medical men say to the contrary, I believed, and still believe, that many more
people are buried alive than is commonly supposed.
She held fast to that article of my faith; and though,
when I reasoned with her upon the subject, pointing
out the danger of my braving popular prejudice in
order to carry her wishes into effect, she relinquished
the idea of being dissected, it was only with the proviso that she should be opened after death, and I be
witness to the operation.   Nothing but a direct pro-

mise to that effect would satisfy her. My word was given and kept. I shall, perhaps, be blamed for this. It may be said that allowing the body to be opened was bad enough, but for a man to stand by and see the dissecting knife used upon her who had been his first love, was in the highest degree criminal. But it should be remembered I was a freethinker, and free-thinking had taught me to conclude that we cannot better show our respect for the dead than by fulfilling to the very letter their latest injunctions while living. The habit of thinking freely on all matters had also led me to the conclusion that the dead are truly " but as pictures ;" a corpse being no more a human being than the soil of the Nile is the serpent which crawls upon its banks. My wife was dead, and, to borrow the emphatic words of Shakespeare, nothing could touch her further. I confess that in complying with her singular request, my bosom's lord did not sit lightly on his throne; but this I know, the request was complied with under the influence of feelings and motives pure as honorable. To my astonishment, however, I soon discovered that my gossipping neighbours were dreadfully shocked at my " inhuman " conduct towards " a poor dead wife." The female part of them were, as usual under such circumstances, the least reasonable and most noisy. A writer who knew women well, declared them worse and better than we are. When evilly inclined I have ever found them the wickedest of God's children. No sooner did it get abroad that I had stood by, seemingly quite calm, while the surgeon operated upon my deceased wife, and, shocking to confess, had sacrilegiously complied with his desire to have her heart preserved as a curiosity, (it having swollen to an extraordinary size,) than all the gin-drinking fanatical beldames and credulous gossips in enlightened Westminster set their tongues to work so effectually, that before the day of interment I was magnified into a rare monster. Their tale, like idle tales in general, lost nothing by the carriage, and at last bore about the same kind of likeness to the original that the famous one about an unfortunate who had vomited three black crows did to the simple circumstance that somebody somewhere had discharged from his stomach something as black as a crow. Not till after the funeral was I made sensible of the very dangerous position in which I had been placed. It then came out that a band of the female furies above mentioned intended to lay violent hands on me, and would have done it in the churchyard but that a detachment of police were on the spot. What brought them there, who sent them, or, if sent, for what purpose, I cannot tell. The most probable of all conjectures is, that the women kept their secret so well, that the authorities became informed of their intentions, and properly (I think) took measures to frustrate them.

Daniel O'Connell once observed, that if he wished to keep anything a profound secret, he would publish it in the Dublin Gazette. Such a way of keeping a secret, though Irish in appearance, is really as good as would that of entrusting it to the careful keeping of gossiping women, who are never at home except abroad, and for the life of them cannot be without an interesting tale of some sort. To the police, then, I owe much—perhaps my life; as from the temper displayed by the ladies, who had agreed to avenge the outrage committed upon one of their sex, they were evidently bent on making a " sky farmer" of me. Our police when wanted are said to be invisible blues; but I protest against the slander; for, as already intimated, had they been invisible blues when *I* wanted them, it it is very likely these Confessions never would have been written; nothing being more improbable than that their author should have penned them, if thirteen or fourteen years ago, like Orpheus, he had been torn to pieces by women. Had I one tithe the presumption of artful priests, this NARROW ESCAPE would be ascribed to Providence, not the Police—to the finger of God not the hand of Man.

CHAPTER XI.

DESPERATE RESOLVE.

IN the spring of 1835, Lord Melbourne's ministry suspended the Foreign Enlistment Act. Their object was (very much to the annoyance of my Lord Londonderry and other conservative statesmen who favoured Don Carlos) to aid her "august" majesty, Isabella of Spain. At that period her cause had received heavy blows and sore discouragement at the hands of Zulamacarregui. The armies of her majesty had been beaten at all points by that famous chieftain. Our Whig rulers were alarmed; they felt that their own existence as a ministry depended in part, if not wholly, upon the turn taken by affairs in the Peninsula. It was clear that if unaided by foreign troops Isabella Segunda would be precipitated from her throne, and absolutism once more triumph in the person of Don Carlos. At every hazard they determined to prevent this. They found, as cautious Sir Robert would say, three courses open to them; one was to let the belligerent parties fight it out, unaided and unopposed; another was directly to make war upon the Carlists; the third was to do the same thing *in*directly. This last named course it was they determined to pursue. Recruiting for armies to serve under foreign governments was forbidden by the terms of the Foreign Enlistment Act; by suspending its operation for two years they in effect said to the tottering Spanish government—Assist you openly and directly we dare not, such policy might cost us our places; but covertly and indirectly we will help you to an Auxiliary Legion of genuine "Britishers," who will fight for her majesty the Queen or his majesty the Devil, if well paid for fighting. Terms were agreed on, abundance of money promised, some fools with a considerable number of rogues enlisted, and the famous British Legion formed—to the exceeding great joy of Lord Palmerstone, and disgust of absolutists all the world over. On the poor Legion these people exhausted the vocabulary of vituperation. They were not only disgusted with its formation, but the " material " of wheih it was composed. On hearing their piteous lamentations, one might have imagined that "playing at soldiers" was a game only "respectable" people should be engaged in. . That the British Legion was not the *most* respectable body of heroes is quite true. A noble peer described them as the sweepings of our large towns, against which sweeping description I have not one word to say. To my knowledge the Legion was, in great part, composed of bankrupt tradesmen, ruined reprobates, broken-down dandies, discharged lunatics, refractory paupers, and sturdy beggers, who, full of patriotism, "left their country for their country's good." Add to these—multitudinous striplings, "seeking the bubble reputation even in the cannon's mouth," unlucky seducers, more fearful of parish officers than Spanish Carlists,—half-pay officers, and scions of aristocracy, devoured by *ennui* (who deemed cutting a throat not too heavy a price for strong excitement),—crazed lovers, anxious, but unable, to get married,—tired-out husbands, anxious, but unable, to be single,—and you have the "material" out of which arose, as if by magic, the famous British Legion. With what sort of armed men Cadmus was rewarded, when he sowed the earth with dragon's teeth, historians do not tell us; but, I imagine, they were *very* respectable in comparison with General Evans' corps. Perhaps Sir John Falstaff's ragged regiment, marching through Coventry, presents a picture most resembling the ragged Legionaries marching through our towns and cities.

Disgusted with the past, and ill at ease with the present, so favorable an opportunity to leave my native land was a "God send." The death of my wife left me once more free to act. Let me here confess that though losing her caused me some grief, regaining my freedom caused me more joy. Our re-union rendered less painful, perhaps, but failed to heal the wound she had so wantonly inflicted. Like Mercutio's, 'twas past all surgery; and, in my heart of hearts, I felt the truthfulness of that part of a modern play which says—*Where convenience and fair appearance, joined to folly and ill-humour, forge the fetters of matrimony, they gall with their weight the wedded pair.* On her side, it was all for *convenience;* and duped by the *fair appearance* she assumed, no wonder that I longed to shake off the *galling fetters* of matrimony,—no wonder that at her death, like Macbeth, when relieved from the presence of blood boltered Banquo, I said, "*Why so; being gone, I am a man again.*"

An ancient sage, asked by some love-sick youth about the wisdom of marriage, assured him it *was* quite immaterial whether he married or not: if you marry, quoth the sage, you will repent,—if you do not marry you will repent. Bachelors are best able to say whether those who *do not* marry repent. Many of them look as if they repented in something worse than sackcloth and ashes. As regards those that *do not* marry, per-haps, few repent, except certain unfortunates, who, like myself, have found the fetters of ma-trimony forged for them by convenience and fair appearance. It is probable all such will sympathize with, and make excuses for, the Con-fession that my wife's death caused me more joy than sorrow, and that when all was over I felt greatly relieved. To recall the past was impossi-ble—a past that embittered the present, and cast a veil over the future. Had she lived I never could have been happy with her. But, though pleased to escape the hateful thraldom into which fate plunged me, my pleasure was—past descrip-tion—melancholy. Before marriage I was ac-counted "a fellow of infinite jest,—of most excellent fancy;" and poor Yorick himself could hardly have better succeeded in setting "the table in a roar." After marriage, but especially at the time I entered the British Auxilary Legion,

my mirthfulness forsook me and my temper
grew sour. The Narrow Escape referred to in
my last chapter, though a trifle in itself, caused
my cup of wretchedness to overflow. All things
seemed destined to blast my peace. A disposition, naturally benevolent, threatened to become
morbidly misanthropic. Women I regarded
with contemptuous pity; and "troops of friends"
as objects of suspicion who, in all probability,
would one day become my enemies. Like
Goldsmith's hermit I could say, with *bitter*
sincerity,

> What is friendship but a name,
>   A charm that lulls to sleep,
> A shade that follows wealth or fame,
>   And leaves the wretch to weep.
>
> And love is still an emptier sound,
>   The modern fair one's jest;
> Not seen on earth, or only found
>   To warm the turtle's nest.

In this uncomfortable state of mind, I determined
to leave the shores of my *then* detested country;
and though "the trade of war" was not the one
which, under happier circumstances, I should
have chosen, yet a soldier's life, at that critical
period of my history, seemed to me not altogether without its charms. As already intimated,
to mend, or be rid of, my life, I was resolved.
1 did not, like Childe Harold, feel *pleasure drugged*
and therefore *long for woe*, having had more than
enough of it; but, like him, should hardly have
objected *e'en for change of scene to seek the shades
below*. Nor did soldiering for a shilling, a six-
pence, or even (as was frequently my case) nothing a day, appear so horrible a crime against
philosophy, and morality, as certain Quakerly
people seem to think it. Common soldiers I
knew where looked upon with abhorence, even
by those who, without common soldiers, would
cease to exist, except in a state of common serf-

dom ; but to me there appears nothing disgraceful in the act of becoming a common soldier.
Cervantes, the immortal author of Don Quixote,
was, at one period of his life, a common soldier ;
so was Cobbet, the terror of political quacks ;
and after Paine, the raciest and most powerful
of political writers.

Many people think I went to Spain solely
actuated by a noble desire to combat on the side
of liberty ; but they are deceived. I joined the
Legion with the hope of bettering my condition,
through some lucky accident, or some bold *coup
de main*. This abnegation of self, at the shrine
of liberty, is one of the virtues with which I have
been unjustly credited. It is true that I preferred
even the pseudo-liberalism of Queen Isabella to
the monkish absolutism of Don Carlos, and at
another time might have taken a higher than
any selfishly personal interest in the struggle.
Love of travel was strong within me. By join-
ing this Legion, thought I, my passion for travel
may be gratified at the expense of her exalted
majesty, the Queen of Spain. Dislike of England, and the English,—a feeling intimately associated with mortified vanity and disappointed
ambition, was another of the low motives by
which I was actuated in this DESPERATE
RESOLVE. Some importance consequences of
my rashness will be enlarged upon in another
chapter,

CHAPTER XII.

MILITARY EXPERIENCE.

IT is not my intention to weary the reader with a detailed account of "the battles, sieges, fortune, that I passed" in the Peninsula. Such reminiscences seem to me the reverse of either pleasant or glorious; but, without *some* account of them, these Confessions would be found wanting, and fail to satisfy the curious. I was there about two years, having embarked in that crazy old hulk, the Lord Lyndoch, from the Isle of Dogs, on the 24th July, 1835, and disembarked from a brig, hired to convey Legionaries from Spain, at Portsmouth, on the 22nd July, 1837. During that period, which to me appeared an age, I became acquainted with many truths the romance writer would deem invaluable, as they are really stranger than any ordinary fiction, and the hero of many events which, thrown into a dramatic form, and produced at the Victoria, would make the fortune of the Lessee of that exciting place of amusement. The troubles of myself and companions commenced early, for off the coast of France our vessel ran upon some rocks which a dense fog had hidden from view. The crash was dreadful, and no less so were the shrieks of women, assisted by the squalling of children and riotous frenzy of men, many of whom, though old soldiers, betrayed a fearfulness as absurd as it was unmanly. What added to their terror was the uncertainty in which they were for a long time kept as to the condition of the vessel. It struck about four o'clock in the morning,—a time when all the Legionaries were down below, and the captain prudently ordered that below

they should remain till the danger was past.
Never shall I forget the countenances of those
people.   Men, women, and children huddled
together, regardless of every thing but their own
safety, is not a sight calculated to inspire much
respect for one's fellow creatures.   At that trying moment I stood calm as a statue, thinking
of Byron's line—

Now shrieked the timid and stood still the brave.

It occurred to me then, and I have seen no
reason to alter the opinion since, that in such
scenes calmness is the best evidence of courage.
My calmness did not proceed from contempt of
death, but from the well grounded conviction
that, in circumstances of danger, sighs, tears,
and groans avail nothing.   Assuredly rocks are
neither to be removed nor softened by them.
Escape we did, in some marvellous manner
that no one seemed able to explain ; and, after
sailing a few more days, we found ourselves within sight of Spain.   What I suffered, in that beautiful but misgoverned country, no language can
describe, compelled, as I was, for two long years,
to consort with the most disgusting wretches ;
and, at word of command, to march forth with all
the pomp of streamers and trumpets, to shoot at,
or bayonet, men, of whom I knew nothing, and
from whom I had received no injury.   My feelings
were of the most painful description sometimes,
indeed so painful that the idea of committing
self-destruction often obtruded itself upon my
diseased imagination.   Let those who can delight
in the pride, pomp, and circumstance of glorious
war—I am unable to do so.   My Spanish campaign effectually cured me of all admiration for
such atrocious follies.   To give a detailed account
of that campaign, is, as already observed, no part
of my present plan.   Confessions, such as these,
cannot conveniently be crowded with details, nor

is it necessary they should be so. A relation of
one or two circumstances will suffice to show the
straits to which I was reduced and hopeless
misery of my situation. While the legion were
operating on the heights of Arlaban, near Vit-
toria, I was prostrated by fever, and conveyed
to a military hospital. How the patients were
attended to there, may be judged from the fact
that that duty was done (after a fashion) by soldiers of the Legion, who were for the most part
low bred scheming ruffians, capable of any atro-
city, who, having schemed themselves into hospital, determined to stick there and turn their
position to account. Many of them did so to an
extent almost incredible. While poor patients
wanted the necessaries of life, those wretches
were feasting like princes. Drunkenness was
the order of every day. Responsibility there
was none. Each member of the hospital staff
did what seemed right in his own eyes. Con-
signed to their tender mercies for six weeks, the
sufferings I experienced from dirt, from cold,
from vermin, and poisonous food, will not be
soon forgotten. I was long a prey to raging
fever. In a state semi-delirious I lay for weeks
stark naked, on a hard narrow mattrass, between two other sufferers as naked as myself.
Being for upwards of a fortnight worse than
either of my wretched companions (both of
whom subsequently died), I was placed in the
middle, on my back, whence I could not move
without assistance ; and they were obliged, so
narrow was the mattrass, to lie on their sides.
We all preferred being naked to wearing our
shirts, in the coarse seams of which millions
of lice did congregate and torment us. They
were of all colours ; and adhered to one's
skin, with the tenacity of leeches. Rats, too,
abounded in that horrible place. Their size and
boldness equally astonished me. A whole army
of them would sally forth, from their holes, at

night, and fall to work upon whatever they could
find, with the voracity of famished wolves. At
the time to which I refer, in consequence of
general hard usage and poison administered to
them in bread, furnished to the Legion by a baker
sold to Don Carlos, our men died, with fearful
rapidity. Daily holes used to be dug, into which
six, eight, sometimes a score, of naked carcases
were thrown. But it frequently happened that
the rats attacked the still palpitating flesh of the
dead ; and, before ought was known or cared
about it, helped themselves to a hearty meal.
Even the living were not safe in the presence of
those fierce creatures ; for whom, as mentioned
in a former chapter, I always felt peculiar aversion. Judge then, reader, what my state of mind
must have been, when night after night, partially
devoured by fever, I expected to be entirely
eaten up by a *posse* of rats, the least of which
seemed larger than many full grown kittens. In
those bitter moments it was not death that
alarmed me, but the probable manner of dying.
I can well remember wishing for death ; and
even deriving satisfaction from the thought that
my hour had almost come. It is strange, passing
strange, how the mind adapts itself to circumstances. While in health, and breathing the free
air of liberty, the idea of dying in a foreign land,
tormented and threatened by vermin, without a
friend to cheer my heart or close my eyes, would
have been unspeakably agonizing to me, but the
reality was not. Out of Pandoras box flew all the
evils of life ; but hope was left at the bottom.
By the worst evils of life I was sorely afflicted.
but hope did not forsake me : it was still at the
bottom of the box,—not hope that I should
recover (as for weeks no such hope was cherish-
ed), but hope that my end would be speedy and
pleasant. One reflection disturbed me very
much. In consequence of being constrained to
lie constantly on my back, the bones gave evi-

dence of an intention to burst through the skin.
I remembered that my brother Edward had some
years before died at Brighton of consumption ;
and notwithstanding the softness of the bed on
which he lay and the care of his nurse, his back
bones actually protruded through the skin before
his death. Now, the reflection which most disturbed my equanimity was, that long before able
to die my fleshless bones would be brought into
agonizing contact with the wretched pallet on
which my fate had thrown me. Obviously, however, I was not fated to feast either Spanish rats
or Spanish worms. Notwithstanding the pitiable plight in which I found myself, and notwithstanding the doctor's decided opinion that it
was all over for me, as far as regarded *this*
world at all events, I recovered, returned to
perform military duty, and actually did take
part in many a bloody fray. Upon such scenes I
have not space, neither have I least inclination,
to dwell. They are passages in the life of a free,
or any other, thinker, unworthy to be revealed.
It is sufficient to say that my two years in Spain
was so prolific of sharp misery as almost to blot
out the recollection of all I before had endured.
Even at this distant period I cannot think of it
without a shudder. During that terrible two
years, I was often so demonized by hunger that
the smallest loaf would have been held to be
cheaply paid for by the life of an innocent fellow
creature. Killing did not then appear to me in
the light of murder ; and, let moralists say what
they please about stern virtue and rigid adherence to just principles, *very* hungry people
pay no regard to one or the other. The daintiest
epicure, rather than starve, has been known to
eat the flesh and drink the blood of his companion. Hunger drives men mad ; and the
hungry never will pay much regard to human
life. I have been three whole days on a few
scraps of hard biscuit and a few draughts of cold

water. At the end of that time I have felt " as if all hell were in my heart and I in hell." Of what value did fine moral high-sounding principles then appear to me? Not any. I felt the vulture knawing at my heart; and to appease that vulture (*if undeterred by fear*) would remorselessly have sacrificed whole hecatombs of fellow creatures. But I have said enough, perhaps more than enough, about my Military Experience, every considering student of which will be tempted, as I have often been, to exclaim with the poet—*Oh! what a devil's a man when he forgets his nature.*

CHAPTER XIII.

FIRST LECTURE.

AFTER campaigning, in the miserable manner described in my last chapter, I found myself once more walking the streets of London, not a sadder but assuredly a wiser man. Never before had the great metropolis appeared so beautiful in my eyes. All was *couleur de rose*. I had walked from Portsmouth with only fourteen or fifteen pence in my pocket; and, as can easily be imagined, felt greatly fatigued on my arrival at Westminster Bridge; but neither fatigue nor what is worse perhaps—an empty pocket, could repress feelings the most intensely exquisite I ever experienced. What pious pilgrims feel on reaching the tomb of Christ I know not; but much question that even they feel emotions more joyous than those which shook my whole frame, as a reed is shaken by the wind, when, after an absence of two years, I stood within the centre recess of Westminster Bridge, and, with what Wordsworth might call a *superstitious* eye of love, gazed on the wonders of old father Thames. To me they then appeared passing wonderful. After a ten minutes pause there, I determined that the prodigal should first honour with a visit his more fortunate brother William, then foreman and contractor for the Messrs. Broadwood alluded to in a former chapter. He had no suspicion that I was so near him. On the contrary he believed me dead ; and, except from the grave, never expected a visit from me. I say except from the grave, because often before my Desperate Resolve to a go a soldiering, we had argued about the possibility or probability of ghosts, or other shadowy travellers from the world of shadows, re-visiting this world ; and each pledged himself, if he died first, to come back just to pay his brother a visit, and, partiality at least, let him into the " grand secret," if the the thing *could* be done. When, therefore, after a silence of many months, during which period no tidings of me could be obtained, I suddenly appeared before my brother, that he should conclude I had come straight from the world of spirits in fulfilment of our compact was not surprising. To be sure I did not look very like a ghost, being dressed, *a la mode Francaise*, in clothes purchased of a fashionable Spanish tailor, and displaying cheeks with far more flesh and colour, than any genuine ghost was ever known to exhibit. Nevertheless my brother's first impression was that not I, but my spirit, had honoured him with a visit. After convincing him that I was myself and "no mistake," he took me to his elegant home in the Edgeware Road, where no fatted calf was killed and served up, but a capital dish of steaks was ; and, my appetite being keen, almost beyond endurance, I ate one of the heartiest, best enjoyed meals, I remember at any time to have

eaten.   In less than a fortnight I was once more
at Broadwood plying my " detested" trade ; but
though my dislike to building piano-fortes was
invincible, I went to work with pleased alacrity,
and a firm resolution to put money in my purse
by what mechanics call making up for lost time.
My exertions were prodigious.   I set to work
with the same sort of fury that renegades usually
display when attacking opinions they formerly
entertained.   My brother no longer complained
that I did not do enough work, but that I did
too much.   My circumstances became "easy;"
and a love of hard work, for the sake of what
hard work would bring, supplied the place of
every other.   In order to gratify this new-born
avarice, I resolved " to scorn delight and live
laborious days;" but that resolution, so virtuous
in appearance, yet so ignoble in its source, soon
yielded to the force of circumstances totally un-
forseen.   With a view to economy, as well as
either instruction or amusement, I attended a
variety of debating clubs, the greater part of
which were strictly private.   At those clubs all
sorts of questions, religious, scientific, and political, were discussed.   In some of them, members
constantly protested against meddling with
theology, and as constantly did the very thing
against which they protested.   I used to enjoy
the fun of hearing a speaker, who would set out
by deprecating anything like controversy on religious or theological matters, and sit down, after
delivering a long-winded speech, three-fourths
of which had reference to theology and nothing
else.   Such ridiculous inconsistency is hard to
be avoided by men who have an itch for talking
politics without reference to religion, as if the
two were not in reality the same *one* thing.   The
Illiad without Achilles, or Hamlet without the
Prince of Demark, would be no less satisfactory
than a theory of politics from which religion
should be excluded.' It is religion which leaveneth

the whole lump of human society; and he is a shallow politician who would reconstruct society without knowing what kind of leaven the religious leaven is. But, as before said, the members of debating clubs, I have had the honour to "spout" in, however little disposed for theological controversy, were sure to indulge in it. No matter what was the question under debate, in nine cases out of ten religion was brought upon the carpet. I took part in all sorts of debates, generally in the character of an opener, and soon established for myself the dangerous reputation of being a ready man and a fluent speaker, but cursedly sarcastic. That reputation sticks by me, notwithstanding the pains I take to get rid of at least a portion of it.

Having, in connexion with these clubs, become *tres distingue* a sort of Triton among the Minnows, my ambition was satisfied; but I was destined to play a part rather more conspicuous than that. At the time I was thus doing the Mirabeau on a small scale, Mr. Hollick, a Socialist missionary, who had created some stir by the delivery of Lectures in the metropolis, was called into the country. He had been announced to deliver a Lecture on the Production and Distribution of Wealth on the evening of the day he set out. It happened that that very evening I was present at a debating club, held in the Westminster Road. Thither the disappointed committee who had engaged Mr. Hollick to Lecture, at the well known institution at the corner of Hercules Buildings, Lambeth, came to me, and asked, as a special favour, that I would deliver the Lecture announced by Mr. Hollick. In vain I pleaded want of time for preparation, and want of ability even though time were allowed, to stand before a public audience, and deliver myself satisfactorily on so grave an occasion and so important a subject. The committee insisted upon it that I was a very

clever fellow; and, they convinced me of the
pleasing fact, or at least they convinced me
that Charles Southwell was a cleverer fellow
than he ever before had suspected himself to be.
So away I went, mounted the platform with an
agitated brain and palpitating heart, delivered a
Lecture on the Production and Distribution of
Wealth, not one word of which do I now recollect; and, not one word, am I anxious that
any body else should take the trouble to recollect
for me.   It was a capital Lecture no doubt; for
every body applauded it, and what every body
applauds must be good.   So highly did the relieved committee appreciate my exertions on
that interesting occasion, that I was forthwith
requested again to astonish the natives by my
eloquence.   I did so; and soon found myself
ranked amongst the great guns of Socialism.
Many professed to prefer me to any other
preacher and teacher of Socialism.

But if my speeches, "in temples made with
hands," caused a sensation amongst the friends,
my open air discourses on Kennington Common,
created an absolute *furor;* and, certainly as
regards open air preaching, in advocacy, but
more especially defence of rationalistic principles, no man of this generation has been so
successful as myself.   I am good at manageing
crowds, and the larger the crowd the more
successful is my management of it.   When, therefore, admirers say I am cock of this particular
walk, my innate modesty does not prevent me
from owning " the soft impeachment." Believing
myself nothing less, I am not ashamed to crow
about it. Christians, falsely so called, who have
helped the Lord by preaching "furious and
fact," on Kennington Common, every Lord's
day, for some years past, will never forget the
castigations received at my hands.   They dread
me most dreadfully.   My very name suffices to
throw them into " admired disorder;" and when,

as it happened a few weeks since, I pay a visit to Kennington Common, the scene of former glories, my appearance is the signal for the scattering of their flocks and herds. My gospel shop is no sooner opened than their gospel shop closes, from sheer want of customers. Preaching, in the open air, may be very well; but these Aminidab Sleeks who preach the word, dont fancy pouring their "incomprehensible truths" and "unsearchable riches" *to* the open air. For their comfort I will add, that my last visit to Kennington Common, in all probability, was my last visit in more than one sense. Open air preaching, though very much to my taste, is very injurious to my health; and, after the experience I have had of the people, I do not feel the least inclination to be a martyr in their cause. Let those who covet the crown of martyrdom wear it. They will not find me envying them the possession of a bawble so unpleasant to sense and so questionable to reason.

CHAPTER XIV.

MISSIONARY EXPERIENCE.

AFTER a month's "talking" on my own account, sometimes all for love and sometimes all for hire, I was duly appointed a Socialist Missionary. At that time, towards the close of 1839 or beginning of 1840, the Socialist party had increased—was increasing, and the Bishop of Exeter (ever riding whirlwinds if not directing storms) thought should be diminished. With a view to its di-

minution, he made a fierce attack on Socialism
and Socialists, in the House of Lords, which, to
to say the least of it, was highly imprudent;
but the party, at whom the blow was aimed,
had not wisdom enough to take advantage of
their adversary's mistake.   On the contrary,
they made a still greater.   Instead of resisting
the Bishop's attack, in a manly spirit, they or
rather their Executive, who so admirably mis-
managed their proceedings, by warning Missionaries to be guarded in their language,—to
refuse answering any but written questions after
the delivery of a lecture,—to respect prejudices
and avoid irritating subjects of controversy,—
plainly showed the " white feather."   Just when
a bold front might have been shown, this set of
incapables were shivering with fright; and, at
the shrine of their own pale spiritedness, were
sacrificing the fairest hopes of Socialism.   Disgusted with them and their policy, I condemned
both ; and, to this hour, I have believed the
condemnation was just.   Of course my conduct
was laid to the account of factious motives, and
a desire to distinguish myself, the only good
desire they credited me with.   Every part of
their conduct savoured of the calm insolence,
and self-complacent unprincipledness, of a
bearded Methodist Conference,   The *New Moral
World*, called the organ of Socialism, but in
reality the organ of a clique, who usurped all
authority, was chiefly remarkable for its time
serving jesuitical spirit.   None of its articles
astonished by their boldness, or enlivened by
their wit.   The editor viewed it in the light of
a snug little freehold he alone had a right to
enjoy.   He would have no rival near the edito-
rial throne, as if the *New Moral World* had been
called into existence for the sole benefit of
George Alexander Fleming.   Week after week
its columns were crowded with reports, carefully
dressed up by the said magnanimous George

Alexander, from which it appeared that he was the apostle Paul of Socialism, and main pillar of Owenite orthodoxy. Those same columns were hermetically sealed to reports of a different description. The editor cared not how many opinions his correspondents held if they were but unanimous. A wish to alter so contemptible a system was ascribed to factiousness: any attempt to expose the profiters thereby—to envy. The snug little freehold was fortified like some castle in a besieged country, so admirably indeed that the assaulter found himself repulsed on every side. As an instance of this I would mention that at the time Buchanan, a Missionary belonging to the party of order, that is to the party of exclusion and plunder, took certain oaths, with a reservation, in order to safely continue preaching truth without mystery, mixture of error, or fear of man, I, in my character of Missionary, sent a protest for publication in the *New Moral World;* but the cautious Scot, who edited it, objected to insert my protest, on the ground that the "cause" would be injured if Missionaries found fault with each other in view of the public. Well, not succeeding in taking this thing by the head, I seized it by the tail, in other words I wrote another condemnatory protest or letter, and thought to make it safe by getting a friend to copy it, and then to send the copy for insertion as his own. But that move met with no better success, for the editor declined to insert it on the ground that the subject had been sufficiently discussed, though, in point of fact, the subject had not been discussed at all, except we call that discussion which is all on one side.

In the meantime the influence of Socialism became "small by degrees and beautifully less." Its Missionaries treated the public to plenty of pretty small talk about the folly of praising or blaming, and the delightful things that were to be in the parrollellegrammatic paradise; but they made no way. The public had found them out. They stood self-convicted of the most palpable, and, at the same time, contemptible fraud ever palmed by knavery on credulity. The enchantress in Grims's Fairy Tale, refuses to give her daughter to a suitor unless he will agree to do a variety of impossible things: such as dry up the red sea, eat three hundred oxen at a meal, and drink an equal number of barrels of wine just to wash them down. These pitiable Missionaries were like that enchantress; for, though they agreed all men should have paradise, which all were assured was quite within their reach, they made the doing of sundry and several impossible things an indispensable condition on the part of those who *should* get there. What themselves could not accomplish, they insisted upon others effecting. What nobody could do, they declared must be done ere men could be born again, and all go bodily into the "practical" kingdom of heaven. The topmost height of their folly was reached in 1841. Attacked by the Bishop, in 1839, they seemed almost out of their wits; and so continued till the Congress of Manchester, held in 1841, when they seemed actually so, or to write by the card, their wits were out of them,—put to flight,—clean gone. Never shall I forget that funniest of Congresses, not except- ing the very funny Congress, which has just closed its meetings at Frankfort on the Maine. Its members were almost all "back bone" Owen- ites,—men who would swear to the truth of whatever the father of Socialism affirmed, whether what he affirmed were true or not. I doubt if any Pope, either of modern or ancient times, played a more popish part than did Robert Owen at that Congress; and I am sure no Pope ever was surrounded by a set of more abject worshippers. I except myself, in har- mony with the good old rule, that in cases such

as this, present company is always excepted.
The truth is I never could stomach popery of
any sort, kind, or description. Freedom of mind is
the grand desideratum for which I contend. But
the influence of Mr. Owen sat like a night mare
upon the energies of his "disciples." They not
only endured slavery, but actually seemed to
like it. As their master he was willing that all his
disciples should be Kings, but then he was to be
Viceroy over them.

> He gave his little senate laws,
> And sat attentive to his own applause.

Almost the first "great truth" he told this
memorable Congress was, that old things could
not last another month; and, after delivering
himself of that "great truth," he proceeded to
assure the delighted Missionaries that they, and
they only, knew the causes of existing evils;
and that they, and they only, knew how to remedy them. Though myself a Missionary I was
hard of belief: to me it appeared too good to be
true; and I ventured to suggest that, instead of
wasting time on chimerical subjects, we should
employ it in considering how to deal with tangi-
ble and really useful questions. I went on to
say that, in my opinion, the public mind was
not prepared for a total change of society; and
expecting, as Mr. Owen did, to be called in, by
government, to prescribe for all our political
diseases, was expecting foolishly. I added, that
what we really needed was an efficient corp of
Missionaries, whose sole mission should be the
honourable one of preparing the popular mind
for a reception of those truths, without which
Socialism must ever be ranked among the dreams
of dreamy- minded men; and concluded my
speech by saying that, instead of prolonging a
discussion so absurd, the Congress had better set
forth its principles, means, and objects, in an

intelligible form, so that Missionaries might no longer be talking without well understanding what they were talking about,—being furnished by Congress itself with a text book, which every Missionary might accept and be ready to defend. This speech called up **Mr. Owen**, who, petulantly waving his hand, declared I was not a practical man,—that the only practical man was himself,—that, before the lapse of three months, old things would pass away and all become new, and government must call him in to save the sinking state, or rather to create another state upon the parrellellogrammatic principle,—that his book of the *New Moral World* was the only good and perfect book, and, therefore, that Congress should not waste time on anything so superfluous as a text book for Missionaries,—that the time for agitating the public mind was past, and the golden age about to commence. Not exactly convinced by this speech, neither was I to be silenced by it, and at once replied, that I had no desire to waste the time of Congress, or say a word about Mr. Owen's perfect book, or offer any opinion as the coming millennium ; but felt bound to declare that, if Congress granted me a committee of investigation, I would undertake, before that committee, to prove that neither the Rational Religion Society, nor Mr. Owen its founder, had published anything fit to be the text book of any society rational or irrational. Conference decided against my proposal. Its wise, independent, and religiously rational members, were expressive silently ; and, *nemine contradicente* (as far as they were concerned), the "great truth" went forth that Robert Peel, and the other impracticable ministers of the day, would resign forthwith, to make room for Robert Owen and his chosen band of Missionaries (all practical as well as honourable men), whom her majesty, in hot-haste, would instantly send for.

CHAPTER XV.

BRISTOL AGITATION.

On leaving the Congress of wiseacres, whose practical talents and independent spirit were commented upon in the preceeding chapter, I felt that it was "all up" with Socialism. To borrow an expressive theatrical phrase, the thing was damned. I felt that Robert Owen was not the man to do more than talk about regenerating society, and on my arrival at Bristol, where I was sent as Socialist Missionary, I openly avowed these heterodox opinions. The Owenites of that locality were alarmed and scandalized. Questioning the wisdom of their " dear father" was a serious offence in the eyes of these " dear children," who rated me soundly, and exhibited that worst of all rage which grows from fear. No less angry was the Central Board, a body made up entirely of Mr. Owen's creatures. Finding myself in such very hot water,—hopeless of any improvement in the prospects of true Socialism, so long as senseless egotism, in the guise of philanthropy, was the guiding star of *le beau systeme*,—I resigned my Missionaryship,—went, with two others, into business as bookseller, and started the *Oracle of Reason*. One of my partners was William Chilton, a printer, *with* brains ; and John Field, a gentleman who had the misfortune to be *without* any, was the other. Our library was an admirable one,—perhaps the best Freethinkers' library ever known in this country. It contained amongst other scarce works (scarce because dangerous to clerical supremacy), those of Chubb, Tindal, Morgan, Blount, and a host of other Free-thinking thinkers, whose profound thoughts, and quaint, but apt expressions, I hope some day or other to familiarize the public with. Of course, the opening of such a shop, containing such "frightful blasphemy," shocked and frightened, "*rayther*," the sapient magistrates of that godly city rejoicing in the name of Bristol. Like Dogberry, their perfect prototype, they "doomed" us all "to redemption ;" and thought such things "most tolerable and not to be endured." We had occupied the shop about a fortnight when appeared the first number of that terrible print before mentioned. Its appearance made the Bristol Dogberries ten thousand times more fidgetty than they were before. They were agreed as to the absolute necessity of "putting down" a nuisance so dreadful; and immediately on the publication of No. 4, containing the celebrated Jew Book article, I was arrested and conveyed to prison. That article was certainly a provoking one. My object in writing it *was* to provoke; and, with that view, used terms the most offensive I was able to use. After it was composed I read it to my partners, with the distinct understanding that they were if possible to help me to improve it by substituting stronger, or more offensive, language than that used. Few know that that article was written for the noble purpose of testing a great principle and exposing a great delusion. The Bristol Agitation I look back to with pride, because it was carried on for a holy purpose ; and, so far as myself and Mr. Chilton were concerned, with unflinching courage. Had my other partner been as plucky and judicious as Chilton, the Bristol Agitation would have palsied the heart of bigotry, and achieved results second to none in importance for the friends of truth and enemies of sacerdotal humbug.

Immediately after my arrest, bail was offered and refused. The at first refused bail was, however, accepted, on the eigth or ninth day of my imprisonment. But it manifestly appeared, that tke artful Dogberries were very anxious I should not be allowed to go at large till the day of trial, a period of three weeks or more, though I knew not that, nor even suspected it, on the acceptation of my bail and consequent enlargement. He, said a great poet, seldom errs who thinks the worst he can of womankind; and I have had, in many instances, bitter reason to say, and act upon the saying, He seldom errs who thinks the worst he can of *mankind*. It was found that these Bristol magistrates had not determined to accept my bail until measures were concocted by virtue of which they hoped again to lay me by the heels, by entrapping me into the commission of another offence. This was the plot. My partners had, during my incarceration, published copies of the warrant by authority of which I was apprehended, and sold them at a halfpenny each. As they set forth passages from the Jew Book article, they were open to the same objections as that article itself. On my return home, after refreshing myself, I went into the shop, and began selling "blasphemy" as if nothing particular had occurred. Presently in came a clerk, employed in the magistrates' office, for one of the printed warrants. I handed it over to him and received his cash. Perceiving at once the manœuvre of my persecutors, but determined to out manœuvre them, I succeeded in doing so. Assured they would attempt a second arrest, and, as no more sufficient bail could be provided, I should he doomed to suffer three or more weeks of solitary narrow stone cell imprisonment before trial, I resolved not to be arrested, till, as an Irishman *might* say, I gave myself up. To remain in Bristol I saw was useless; and, wishing to eat my Christmas dinner in London, London, thought I, is the place for me. Now it happened that we were provided with a private front door as well as a public front door; and, singularly enough, while the officers sent to arrest me were walking into the public door, I was walking out, in the most private manner possible, at the private door. Having indulged my humour in this matter, I of course indulged my humour by returning to Bristol in time to stand my trial, which took place in January, 1842. On my way to the court public feeling was so strong against me, that stones were hurled by the mob; and I was in eminent danger of being as roughly handled as Haynau, the unlucky Austrian "butcher," was, a few days since, in the city of London, by the rough and ready draymen of Barclay's brewery. The trial lasted two days. Sir Charles Wetherall, who afterwards, "providentially," broke his neck through falling from the box of his carriage, was the presiding judge. Of his conduct towards me I do not complain,—it was quite as good as could be expected from a Christian judge sitting in judgment on an avowed opponent of orthodox religion. To be sure he totally misrepresented my principles, and credited me with the worst motives in his "summing up;" but judges are privileged persons, and not to be judged by reference to such vulgar tests as truth and justice. My defence occupied about ten hours and a half in delivery. In the course of it I observed, more clearly than before, the kind of stuff composing what we complimentarily call popular intellect. I had not spoken an hour before there were outward and visible signs of sympathy on my behalf; and, long before the termination of the first day's proceedings, the judge rose from his seat, and indignantly declared that, unless silence were preserved, he would at once order the court to be cleared. The very people who would have stoned me in the streets were loudly applauding me in the court,—a fact suggestive of the lines put by Shakspeare into the mouth of Coriolanus when that hero is addressing the rabble of Rome,—

> What would you have, ye curs?
> Whose minds do change with every minute,
> And call that noble, which was once your hate;
> That vile, which was your garland.

But, though the populace were affected by my defence, the jury were not, at least not sufficiently affected to brave "respectable people" by pronouncing a verdict of acquital. I was found guilty; and handed over to the tender mercies of my Christian judge, who, after a speech which would have done honour to Bailey or even Jefferies, condemed me to be imprisoned, in the "stone jug" of Bristol, for twelve calender months, and, at the end of that time, to pay one hundred pounds to her most gracious Majesty the Queen. So *light* a sentence was heard with great satisfaction by many, but by none more than by myself, for I fully expected at least twice that term of imprisonment; and, therefore, in my own proper person was a refutation of the old piece of sublimity which says—Blessed is he who expecteth little, finding myself, as I did, on this great occasion, thrice blessed in consequence of having expected too much.

CHAPTER XVI.

PRISON EXPERIENCE.

THOUGH the idea of imprisonment never appalled me, the reality of it I found very unpleasant. My vivacious temper, distaste for restraint, and extreme sensitiveness to whatever is painful, disqualify me for playing the part of a martyr as the part of a martyr ought to be played. Considered in reference to the times in which he lived, perhaps the late Richard Carlisle was the best possible martyr. His power (and a marvellous power it is) to unrepiningly endure imprisonment was immense. A short time before his death he visited me in Bristol Gaol; and, in course of a very interesting conversation, told me that his hours in Newgate were among the happiest he had ever spent. This may be accounted for by reference to the *physique* as well as *morale* of his constitution. His frame was more robust and less disposed to activity than mine. I am one of those who may be fairly classed among atoms on the fidgets: he belonged to the class of stout, stolid, patient reformers, who cannot easily be moved by others, and care little about moving themselves. I speak now in a sense purely physical. Such men, if studious from taste and habit, and able to indulge both freely, care comparatively little for any other kind of freedom. While in Newgate, and even while in Dorchester gaol (where his treatment was much more severe), he was allowed the unlimited use of books, and could carry on his darling paper war with the same facility as if no prison walls inclosed him. I was differently situated, for, although my general treatment

was tolerably good, no books were allowed me
saved those approved by the chaplain of the
goal; and how fastidious and crotchetty he was
may be judged from the fact, that after examining a volume of Senecca's Morals, sent for me by
a friend, he could not "conscientiously" let it
pass, because in the preface thereto, the work
itself was likened to a garden where poisonous
flowers grew side by side with others of a medi-
cinal nature.   Nor was I allowed to correspond
with my friends, unless prepared to allow whatever might be written, either by myself or them,
to be placed under the eyes and judged by this
prejudiced and rather fastidious critic.   As to
writing for the *Oracle of Reason*, or any other
publication, that was "clean out of the way."
My careful keepers would not hear of such a
thing.   Evidently, then, Richard Carlile, enjoyed
advantages which I did not; and, therefore,
could well afford to bear imprisonment more
patiently.   But, though not a model of patience,
though bored almost to death by a stuttering
addlepated chaplain, assisted by a troop of friends
every way worthy of him, my good humour rarely
forsook me ; and, when it did, I am not aware
that any one had the least chance of observing
its flight.   Indeed my character, for all the
virtues under heaven, *save one*, stood, what a
Cockney may be permitted to call, A 1 in the
estimation of those who had the guardianship of
my precious person.   The chaplain declared I was
"a nice young man;" and if christianized a
little would be "a *very* nice young man."   The
governor often favoured me with a visit; and,
many a time, we have enjoyed a hearty laugh
together.   At first the goalers looked upon me as
a dangerous and incurably vicious sort of lunatic,
who should be treated as such lunatics used to
be in the good old times of whips and chains,
when to smother them was considered an act of
mercy.   But after being a few months blessed by

their occasional sweet companionship, the scene
changed, and those very goalers would run to
serve me on the devil-take-the-hindmost principle.   Long before leaving the prison, I every
morning held a *levee*, in grand style, at which
these mollified turnkeys regularly attended,
cheered my nose with snuff, and regaled all my
senses in a variety of ways all highly satisfactory.
Be it noted, moreover, that they did these things
at the eminent hazard of their places, they being
expressly forbidden to hold any other than official
communication with me.   I really do creep into
considerable favour with myself when thinking of
these passages in the life of a Free-thinker ; and
am clearly of opinion, that if snake charmers,
whether of India or elsewhere, are wonderful
people, not less wonderful is the charmer of
Christian turnkeys.

There are flaming Democrats, and hot-headed
Free-thinkers, who when placed in durance vile,
for telling a little too much truth, contrive to
make enemies of all around them.   Kicking
against the pricks is a point of honour with
these parties.   Now with me I confess the point
of honour was more agreeable to the point of
comfort.   But my application of this comfortable
doctrine did not, as already intimated, entirely
succeed with the chaplain, who always viewed
me distrustfully, and showed the *animus*, by
which he was inspired, in his yearly report to the
magistrates on the state of the goal, where, after
alluding to me as a "peculiar" prisoner whose
conversion he had not quite been able to effect,
insinuates that he might have succeeded if I had
been allowed less liberty and my general treatment had been more severe.   Perhaps he thought
what he said ; and. whether he did or not, I can
make due allowance for his position.   This I am
inclined to do for many reasons.   One is, that no
man, in or out of gaol, ever afforded me rarer
sport.   Our day disputes caused me to laugh

half the night. Assuredly they were the funniest specimens of theological and scriptural controversy I ever heard of. Every morning I had the happiness of hearing him stutter through a Bible chapter, and what, in courtesy, I am bound to call a sermon; and every morning, after the sermon, he was anxious to know what I thought about it. Then commenced a discussion, which was carried on smoothly enough for half an hour or so, when, finding himself in a fix, the clerical gentleman would fly into a passion; and, as he stuttered most when most angered, 1 found it difficult to' preserve that respectful gravity of demeanour so desirable under such circumstances. Sometimes he would begin by earnestly calling my attention to the "indisputable" Christian evidences of Christian truth; and when puzzled about them, would jump away to the question of God's existence, saying it was useless attempting to demonstrate the scripture evidences for the benefit of a sinner so hardened as to question the being of a God. At other times he commenced by a cool consideration of that momentous subject; but the moment he found it was easier to assert the existence of something beyond, before, and superior to nature, than to prove it, off he went to the question of evidence, illustrating, in a very amusing way, the old sentence—Out of the frying pan into the fire. He was, in truth, during my thirteen months' imprisonment, quite a martyr to the cause of Christian truth; and, while each succeeding morning I mercilessly roasted him, might have said, with one of the martyrs immortalized in Fox's veracious martyrology,

> This side enough is toasted,—
> Turn, tyrant, then, and eat;
> And see, whether raw or roasted,
> I make the better meat.

The way in which, each morning, after being

toasted and roasted an hour or so, this unlucky
chaplain rushed stuttering out of my cell to cool
himself in the open air, was sufficient to excite
pity in the breast of any Free-thinker less cruel
than myself. Strange to say the old gentleman's
agonies only made me laugh. I have frequently,
after a scene such as here described, laughed no
shorter time than Sir John Falstaff boasted that
he fought. Mirth, so unfeeling, must have proceeded from such principle as actuated Bene-
dict Spinosa (generally the most humane and
excellent of men), when he employed himself in
putting flies into a spider's web, and laughed till
his sides ached, and the tears streamed from his
eyes when the poor fly battled for its life with
the spider. Nor is this the only circumstance
which tends to reconcile me to my cruel dealings
with the chaplain. I draw considerable comfort
from the reflection that the goalers, whose duty it
was to accompany him (a duty due to each in
turn), and remain within ear shot, used to come
back, as soon as able, and fall to laughing as
heartily and as loudly as myself.

It would be wrong did I omit to notice, in
connection with my Prison Experience, an in-
troduction to a Christian gentleman named
Blackwood, for which I was indebted to the
gaol chaplain. He journeyed all the way from
Bridgewater for the avowed, and perhaps real,
purpose of saving my soul. Though a lawyer
he claimed to be considered a good Christian.
Believing him sincere, I received him politely;
and, prior to all discussion, assured him, with
genuine warmth, that if he could "show cause"
for believing his notion of Christianity the
true one, I would willingly renounce my errors
and become "a soldier in Christ." At first, this
limb of the law was courteous and conciliatory;
but, as the discussion waxed warm, he waxed
uncharitable. I found him every inch a lawyer,
though not very skilful in making "the worse

appear the better reason ;" and not so wise as the pugilist who, when asked by a combative young spark which was the best attitude of defence, well replied—To keep a civil tongue in your head. My new friend, Mr. Stevenson Black-wood, when puffed up with conceit and inflamed by opposition, did not always contrive to keep a civil tongue his head. He argued just as some hot-headed lawyer might be expected to argue if under the pleasing impression that he had God his for client and would have heaven for his fee. After three or four set debates, we separated with the understanding that further controversy should be carried on in writing. Accordingly letters were interchanged, one of which so little pleased him that he gave me up for lost ; and sent me a *last* letter which contained a very safe, as well as a very impudent, prophecy, couched in these terms—You, sir, will leave this prison a converted sinner, and monument of the grace of God,—or will leave it a hardened sinner given over to a reprobate mind,—or you will be carried out a corpse with your toes foremost. He was right, of course, for the simple reason that he could not be wrong. No safer prophecy was ever uttered, and no prophecy ever reflected more disgrace upon the prophecier ; but of that each reader will judge for himself.

CHAPTER XVII.

IMPORTANT FACTS.

DURING my imprisonment the periodical, for publishing which I was prosecuted, fell into other hands.   Immediately after my arrest Mr. George Jacob Holyoake, who now occupies so large and honourable a space in the public eye, volunteered to become second priest of the *Oracle;* and admirably did he perform the duties devolving on so exalted a functionary.   I have many times read with pleasure the bold and caustic oracles he pronounced at that dangerous period—oracles equal, in my judgment, to any that ever poured from the mouth of Melchisedeck himself. I pretend not to any *knowledge* of Melchisedeck, or Melchisedeck's oracular effusions; but claiming the license usually allowed only to poets, I *imagine* that his oracles must have been very spicy.   Be this as it may, I consider the oracles of Mr. Holyoake particularly so; and, perhaps, the ablest of all his able works.   They displayed great shrewdness, tact, and knowledge of the world. Others did the oracular occasionally, and with success; but he was the *redacteur en chef,* whilst I was incarcerated: and I take this opportunity to congratulate him upon the capital style in which he carried on the work of " shaking the dry bones of orthodoxy."   The periodical was nevertheless a failure.   From some cause or other it did not pay, in proof of which I need only mention that, on my release from gaol, I found a rather formidable debt had been contracted with a view to its support.   Under these circumstances I declined again to become its responsible editor.   After being imprisoned for principle, I had a natural objection to be imprisoned for debt. Gaping creditors are about the last people on earth I desire to meet. The face of a Gorgon would be less hateful to me than the face of a creditor. This salutary dread of people who want money I owe, but cannot pay, was probably inspired by my remembrance of sufferings endured in youth, which had their origin in embarrassed circumstances.

There were, however, I confess, other than purely monetary considerations which induced me to decline again becoming high priest of the *Oracle*. It seemed to me that the time had come for a periodical somewhat different in its tone, matter, and style; but, if the *Oracle* had proved a paying speculation, it is probable that I might have been induced to resume the management of it. Instead of doing so I started the *Investigator*, which ran through twenty-eight numbers, and then departed in peace. I do not confess to having sent it to the tomb of all periodicals, because its premature death was the fault of others rather than myself. Its printer, who was (or rather ought to have been) also its proprietor, acted in so careless and absurd a manner, that success would have been little short of miraculous. He had too many irons in the fire; and. like most other persons similarly situated, could not keep them all hot. I was the chief sufferer; for, though I wrote nearly everything that was written for and published in the *Investigator*, I did not receive one farthing for my labours. The printer turned bankrupt; and, in consequence, what was due to me remains due to this day, and is likely to remain due till days shall be no more. Henceforth, in dealing with printers, my principle will be—no pay no work. Indeed, my resolution now is, to convince a friend of mine, who frequently says, " Mr. Southwell, whatever other kind of genius you may have, you certainly have not a genius for making money," that he has done me wrong. I confess, that after what I have seen and felt,—after much experience of men, as well as professions or principles, my desire to look after the main chance has wonderfully increased. In the disinterestedness of liberals, especially philosophical liberals, I no longer believe. Declaim, though they may, against selfishness,—and extol, as they may, devotion to principle, the best of them are mere popularity-hunters, whose devotion to principle is at all times less intense than their devotion to cash. I know them well. Their pretensions to disinterestedness are mere humbug. Not one of them, in agitating for the public good, is unwilling to keep a sharp look out for his own interests. There are no Catos now-a-days. We have lots of patriots. You may meet them in every street—hear them in every club—and be stunned, if not astonished, by their eloquence in every public meeting. They are as plentiful as blackberries in blackberry season. But what is got, or to be got, by patriotism, is, with them, the main consideration; and no wonder that it should be so. Patriots must live: other people may see no absolute necessity in the case, but patriots do. What disgusts me is their pretension to disinterestedness, which every experienced politician knows to be a sham. In a former chapter I have declined to take rank among these sham patriots. Accepting that maxim which says--"The labourer is worthy of his hire," I see nothing disgraceful or unworthy of genuine patriotism in demanding hire for *my* labour. Having worked long, far too long, for the benefits of others, I shall, in future, take some little care of myself. On leaving Bristol gaol, after a close imprisonment of more than thirteen months, I found myself in possession of just five shillings, which sum, not being sufficient to defray travelling and other expenses incidental to the proposed journey to London, "my native home," I was obliged to borrow five pounds from a relative, who was not at all anxious to lend. Richard Carlile was supported by money as well as talk. I was supported by talk, and nothing but talk. Agitation never brought grist to my mill; and, while ignorant, low-bred miscreants, such as the " man" Paterson, have been handsomely pursed, my reward has been "apostolic blows and knocks." These things I mention for a public purpose. I neither whine nor complain about them. The friends of Freethinking are at liberty to act as they think fit towards the advocates of Freethinking; but let them not imagine that I feel called upon to make any more sacrifices for a party who never yet sacrificed one iota for me. Since Richard Carlile no man has done so much,—no man *sacrificed* so much the cause of Freethinking,—as myself. Rightly or wrongly I believe this,—rightly or wrongly I publish it,—and rightly or wrongly I assure Freethinkers, that justice never will be done to their principles until something like justice is done to those persons who efficiently advocate them.

Shortly after my return to London I was introduced to the " man" above named. We had never met before. While in prison I received two or three letters from him, which were written in a style so laboured and bombastic that I began to suspect we had picked up a raw recruit for the army of agitation, who had eaten of the insane root which takes the reason prisoner. On seeing this Holywell-street hero, I was not surprised at anything except the vulgarity of his appearance, and awkward attempt to show-off in a part nature never intended him to play. It may be wrong to judge of character from face or figure, but I find myself constantly doing so, and almost as constantly judge righteous judgment. There are, no doubt, many men of vinegar aspect, and sinister look, who belong the class of " jolly good fellows;"

but I never meet with them.   There are certain distinguished men, on every lineament of whose faces scoundrel is written in legible and inefface-able characters.   I *could* mention many such, who at this very time pass for high-minded, honourable, yea, right honourable reformers, but will not do so.   One contents me: Thomas Paterson.   In his face, as in a book, you may read strange matter.   It is the face of a brag-ging, conceited, sensuous, low-minded, but ambitious scoundrel, capable of anything, from picking a pocket to cutting a throat.   How it happened that Mr. Holyoake was so long his dupe and tool, the doer of his dirty work, and voluntary recipient of his insolence, I pretend not to explain.   Paterson is neither a man of talent nor a man of principle; but a needy, brainless, and heartless adventurer, with just enough of learning to misquote,—just enough of low cunning to impose on unsuspecting simple-tons,—and just enough of courage to appear courageous when nothing is to be got by an exhibition of cowardice.   The books ascribed to him were written by others.   His speech before the Scottish Jury who tried him, was prepared by myself.   The book entitled "God *versus* Pater-son" was a concoction of many hands,—of materials from many heads.   This most misera-ble of imposters was incapable either of making a speech fit to be heard, or writing an article fit to be read.   But he had no objection to pick up crumbs that fell from other men's tables; and, like a true jack-daw, would strut about in feathers borrowed from the peacock.   The few articles seemingly furnished by him for the *Movement*, and other periodicals, were not really his; but were furnished by friends who allowed him to append his name to them.   The only article I ever knew him to write was so flagrant an outrage upon all grammar, logic, sense, and his-tory, that the Freethinking party were heartily ashamed, though unable to deny themselves the relief of most heartily laughing at it. *Punch* committed a great sin of omission in not exercising his wit upon it, which I fully expected he would have done. But, strutting about in borrowed plumes, and perpetrating original nonsense, were not the only crimes justly chargeable upon him; for, in many cases, this petty larceny rascal has been known to cut clever things from newspapers and forward them as his own to the *Oracle of Reason* office. An obituary, written on the death of the Duke of Sussex, is an instance of this. It was published in the *Oracle* as Paterson's ; and, when too late, the high priest discovered that the original article had been borrowed from a contemporary. In my next chapter the Scottish Agitation will come under review, and the part played by this vile "man" Paterson so fully exposed, that should he ever again pollute the soil of this country with his presence, no Freethinker, who reads these Confessions, will ever be found in any way countenancing so detestable a miscreant.

CHAPTER XVIII.

SCOTTISH AGITATION.

IN the autumn of 1843, Mr. Robinson, a bookseller of "sweet" Edinburgh, was indicted for selling blasphemous and indecent publications. Exactly at the same time I was preparing for a journey to Scotland, in order to fulfil an engagement entered into with the Socialists of that celebrated city. It happened that a meeting was held, by the London enemies of persecution, on behalf of Robinson, the night before my departure. I attended that meeting,—spoke to a resolution,—and was about to leave the platform, when the man Paterson, who, for weeks before had been extremely cold and distant in his manner towards me, said he wished to have a little conversation. I was much surprised, but immediately said—very well, be it so. He then proceeded to say, it was probable I might be able to find employment for him in Scotland, seeing the agitation like to be consequent upon the arrest of Robinson. I replied that it was next to certain that a man, bold enough to beard the bigots, would be wanted; and, if he were prepared to do so, I would use my influence on his behalf. After he had reiterated his wish to be so employed, we parted; and, as anticipated, I had not been long in Edinburgh before the place became too hot to hold the bigots, and our party wanted a man to take care of a "blasphemy shop" they were about to open in West Register Street. I at once named Paterson as a fit and proper person for the work; for, notwithstanding the unpleasant impression produced upon me by a first view of his "ugly mug," and his subsequent general conduct, I thought him valiant, sincere in his warfare with intolerance, eager for the fray, and altogether a far better man than I afterwards found him. In a Preface to "The Trial of Thomas Paterson," Mr. Holyoake makes it appear that it was not my going to Scotland which led to Thomas Paterson's going there; but the going to Scotland of Thomas Paterson, which led to my going there. This is not the only mistake made in that Preface, which is as curious a piece of history as any I ever met with in all my reading. Well, the "man" joined me in Scotland, and the work of agitation was carried on in a style never before attempted there. For a few weeks Paterson behaved remarkably well,—at the end of that time he began to exhibit the hideous features of his character,—and more hideous features no Gorgon ever had. Night after night was he seen drunk in the open streets. Whilst intoxicated he was brutal in the extreme, and would not only consort with the lowest prostitutes, in the lowest brothels, but actually converted the Scottish Freethinkers' shop into a brothel. Upon one occasion, after luring an unfortunate woman in, and having commerce, he refused to pay the trifle he had agreed to pay. The woman insisted upon an equitable adjustment. Police were called in, and there was what is commonly described as " the devil to pay;" and all this was done under the eyes of the magistrates, who of course were duly informed about the strange doings of "infidel" Paterson. But not content with freaks like these, he took into keeping, or was taken into keeping by a strange, semi-idiotic woman named Nullan, who lived with Paterson and his boon companion, a young man named Bridge—between whom it is supposed she shared her favours.

These excesses and brutalities were indulged in by Paterson, while an indictment for blasphemy, like the sword of Damocles, was suspended over his head. Even after his arrest, and he was admitted to bail, the same scenes of drunkenness and debauchery were nightly enacted. A few days before his trial he was totally unprepared with anything in the shape of a defence. All was dealt with upon the principle of "Come day, go day, God send Sunday." Three days before that important event, he sought me to ask if I would prepare a defence for him. Respect for the principles at stake, and not respect for him, induced me to comply with his request. But, in complying, I had undertaken an incon-

venient as well as difficult task ; for the following evening I had engaged to deliver in Glasgow
the first of three lectures to be delivered on suc-
cessive evenings.   Clearly then the only course o-
pen to me was the very inconvient one of scrawl-
ing out a defence in Glasgow, and forwarding it,
bit by it, to Edinburgh.   All people I have the
honour to correspond with know that my up-
strokes and down-strokes, pot-hooks, hangers,
&c., are sometimes as hard to be deciphered as
the half-defaced hieroglyphics of an Egyptian
temple.   When scribbling for printers, I usually
endeavour to console them by the just reflection
(though a rather paradoxical one), that the
worse I write the better what I write is written.
As might have been expected from so fashionable a writer, who had to commit his thoughts to
paper almost with the rapidity of "greased lightning," a great deal of the defence, posted from
Glasgow to Edinburgh, was unintelligible, or at
all events only to be made out by people in
their sober senses.   Now, it happened that Paterson, and the nice youths he employed to help
him in copying from the sheets as they were
forwarded, drinking nothing but whiskey could
think of nothing but whiskey: all which resulted
in such a manuscript as people, on their trial
for blasphemy, have seldom the misfortune to read
from.   In a report of the trial which appeared
in an orthodox Scotch newspaper, it was remarked that Paterson seemed to have some
difficulty in reading his own defence, which
stimulating the reporter's curiosity, he peeped
over the defendant's shoulder, and saw clear
evidence that the defence had been written in
many hands.   Without doubt the "man" Paterson was awkwardly placed on that occasion, so
awkwardly, that even I felt a sort of contemptuous pity for him: but his punishment was
just.   He had no right to trifle with the advocacy of a great public principle.   He had no

right, by conduct which would disgrace a Caliban, to draw down odium on the heads of his friends. The truth is, he cared neither for friends nor enemies: the only thing on earth he cared for, was himself. His connexion with the Scottish agitation was fatal to it. Of course, he was found guilty of blasphemy, and sent for fifteen months to Perth Penitentiary. I remained in Scotland some months; but, disgusted with Paterson, and also with Robinson, who pleaded guilty to an indictment charging him with wickedly publishing indecent and blasphemous works, I sickened of agitation and agitators. The agitation in reality terminated with the trial of the two worthies just named. On leaving his prison Paterson employed himself in concocting scurrilous pamphlets, which are incomparable specimens of low ruffianism and reckless lying. In one of them, he not only abused me in the High Toby style, which I could well bear, but made a foul attack upon my second wife, one of the best women one earth; and one from whom he had received no injury, but, on the contrary, a vast deal of disinterested kindness. By that act he forfeited all claim to mercy at my hands; and when I take that act, in connection with his many other scandalous crimes, I do feel indignant,—and feel, too, that were his destiny in my hands, his career of infamy would soon be ended. The last intelligence I have had, with regard to him, was through a friend recently returned from America, who said he saw the " man" Paterson there, and that the said " man" had got into trouble. It appears, from his statement, that at the time Paterson landed in America, a dispute about the propriety of abolishing brothels was at its height. An opponent of brothels and brothel keeping, who had greatly distinguished himself, was thought by Paterson a foeman worthy of his steel, or rather a good mark whereat to aim the shaft of calumny. So to work

he went,—started a little trumpery paper, intended to be periodical, in the first and last number
of which he charged the person in question, of
whom, by his own confession, he knew nothing,
with sodomy.   Now, it happens that no American believes, that any American ever did, or
ever will commit that odious crime.   Master Paterson, therefore, was touching on tender ground, ,by wounding the natural vanity
precisely where it was most susceptible.   In
less than an hour after the publication of this
atrocious libel, its author was arrested, carried
to a prison called the Tombs, where he remained
when my friend left America, and where I hope
he will continue for the full term of his abominable life.

It will be remembered that threatening
letters, for the writer of which a reward of £200
was offered, were sent to Mr. Nash, a City
solicitor, on account of his activity in bringing
to justice Maynard and other thieves who had
committed a series of robberies on various rail-
ways.   Paterson, assisted by a married woman
he had debauched, was the writer of those letters.
Facsimiles of them were published in *The Times*,
a single glance at which convinced me they were
written by the vile ruffian I am anxious to expose.
" A fellow-feeling makes us wondrous kind ;" his
wondrous kindness to the thieves, on whose
behalf he threatened Mr. Nash with assassination
if he proceeded against them, may safely be
ascribed to fellow-feeling.   The police having
been informed that I *could* swear to the hand-
writing, I was visited by a superintendent, who
much pressed me to do so; but I declined,
solely because at that time I entertained strong
objections.to oath taking.   If asked now to do
so, I should be less scrupulous.   Two hundred
is a good round sum ; and no man better deserves
transportation, or even hanging, than the miscreant Paterson, who gives the lie to Cobbett's

assertion that "the worst use we can possibly make of a man is to hang him." Before leaving England he subsisted upon the charity of credulous Christians, whose notions of religion he pretended to have suddenly, through God's help, discovered the divinity of. They are heartily welcome to such a convert, and if God, in consequence of hypocrisy so detestable, should have mercy on his soul, I beg it may be well understood that in no case would I have mercy on his body. Mercy to so heartless a ruffian is cruelty to all mankind.

CHAPTER XIX.

FURTHER DISCLOSURES.

IN the preceding chapter incidental mention was made of my second wife; and as nothing was previously confessed, with regard to a second marriage, it is probable that readers will be curious to know a little about so important a circumstance.

While delivering a course of thirteen lectures, I had the good fortune to meet the lady who tempted me once more to encounter the perils of matrimony. She had been induced to hear one of those lectures, which appeared to her rather entertaining, but by no means so entertaining as the lecturer. According to her own account, it was quite an affair of " love at first sight." Quite unconcious of having produced a favourable impression, but struck with her face and figure, on leaving the platform I adopted

the *ruse* of mistaking her for somebody else, and
thereby succeeded in *politely* shaking her by the
hand ; and while apologising for what I feared
might have the air of rudeness, contrived to deliver myself of a few complimentary words.   But
neither on that night, nor till some time afterwards, did I entertain serious thoughts of playing
the lover.   It afterwards appeared that she, on
the other hand, decidedly intended to be loved,
and that I should be the lover.   Knowing that
I was expected at a ball in the building where
we first chanced to meet, she took her measures
accordingly, and great was my surprise, though
not greater than my delight, to find her there on
entering the room.   But the circumstances were
rather awkward, for not at all expecting to meet
her, I had escorted to the ball a fascinating
married lady, with a husband made up of stupid
indifference, and other materials usually entering
into the composition of cuckolds.   I had frequently danced in sweet companionship with this
married lady, who began to look upon me as her
acknowledged *cavalier servente*.   On this occasion
I would willingly have been altogether rid of her :
and after we had danced a few dances I managed
to saddle her upon a friend (friends are very
useful under such circumstances), and went to do
homage at the shrine of my new goddess.   She
was about my own age, above the middle
height, figure admirably proportioned, though
somewhat more than *embonpoint*, large soft blue
eyes, splendid teeth, and features larger than
feminine features usually are, but in their expression decided, firm, voluptuous, but re-
served, and, while radiant with affectionate
intelligence, chaste as those of Diana herself.   Until united to that delightful and
most excellent creature, I never suspected of
how much a loving, generous, high-spirited
woman was capable. *She* was capable of
making any sacrifice, even the sacrifice of life

itself, for the object of her affection ; and if ever
man was adored by one of the other sex, I was
adored by her. We lived together, and for
each other, more than five years, when death
snatched from me the dearest friend and kindest
companion I ever knew. She died of that dreadful disease called cancer—cancer of the uterus.
Oh ! never can I forget the agonies which for
many weary months heralded her dissolution.
Her well knit, powerful, yet tender and beautiful
frame, long resisted the fell disorder, which, like
some fiend, gnawed her inwards. Men say there
is a God. Well, if there is, and that God is just,
he surely will, in some other world, compensate
this martyred woman, the torments by Him inflicted upon her in this. But how compensate. No,
it is impossible : there are agonies, the infliction
of which never can be compensated for. Such
were the agonies she, the finest-hearted, the
noblest specimen of God or Nature's handywork,
endured. To the last, her thoughts were fixed :
her last words were spoken after she had long
been thought incapable of speaking more, and
those words were, " Here he comes, bless his
heart." She uttered them as I entered the chamber, which a few hours more converted into the
chamber of death. What I felt, none can know,
nor is it desirable that any *should* know. There
are griefs too big for utterance—griefs which,
long pent up will burst the heart which is
their prison. Such a grief was mine: not that I
loved her as I thought she deserved to be
loved, or as my nature is capable of loving
an object really in harmony with it. Since
her death, I have loved, do now love, another,
more intensely than I could love her. My
affection for her was stronger than for any
woman that before had crossed my path; but
at this instant I love more intensely and devotedly than till the last two years I thought it
possible to love. My affection for the fair sex

has at all times been strong, but never so strong as now. The poignant grief I felt at the loss of my second wife did not so much proceed from any extravagant affection I felt towards her, as from a deep and abiding sense of her faith, her truth, her intense devotedness, her eminently practical business habits, her lion-like spirit, which forbade insult, and her glorious nobility of soul.

Fortune played me strange pranks during the five years passed in the society of this admirable woman. I never was so poor as absolutely to want a shilling; never so rich as to have £100 at command. In 1844 I took some premises in Charlotte-street, Blackfriars'-road, of the Socialists, who had tried to reform the whole world, and found themselves unable conveniently to raise £50 per annum. I soon altered the aspect of affairs. In less than three months old things had passed away, and all became new. A reform altogether was worked in every department. The lectures drew crowds of listeners, a considerable profit was "realized" through furnishing refreshment as well as amusement; and the Paragon Hall (so the premises were named) turned out a profitable speculation. After some time, finding the place too small, I resolved to enlarge it; and though the space available was not much, contrived to make room for an extra hundred visitors. There was, however, one serious objection to the occupation of such premises, arising out of sanitary considerations. An unhealthier house it would be difficult to select, my health suffering dreadfully during our occupation of it. All the lower part was a dark dark Inferno, scarcely less horrible than Dantes, where one could breathe an atmosphere rendered fœtid and poisonous by bad sewerage, and utter want of ventilation. I would not live there another two years for all the profit to be realized in ten. I had other reasons for leaving besides

those arising out of the state of my health; and
finding a customer for it in the person of W. W.
Brown, better known as " The Coming Axe
Man," I sold the business, and shortly after became lessee of the Canterbury theatre.

It is frequently observed that those who in
youth have a decided taste for the stage, love occasionally to smell the lamps when youth has
passed, and even when time has developed them
into lean and slippered pantaloons. My taste
for acting, exhibited at a very tender age, had
been fostered by my brother Henry, himself
an actor who had occupied a high position at the
Dublin theatre, and also at the Theatre Royal
Drury-lane, who seemed justified by the applause
which invariably rewarded my histrionic efforts.
When I was about twelve years old my brother
left England to fulfil a lucrative engagement in
the United States. From thence he went to the
West Indies, where he built a theatre, and was
running a glorious histrionic career when yellow
fever terminated that fitful fever called life. He
would have taken me with him had I been small
enough for such parts as *Albert*, in *William Tell*,
or large enough for parts requiring people of
adult dimensions. Being

> " A mere hobbody-hoy,
> Neither man nor boy,"

I lost an opportunity—the losing of which has
caused me bitter regret—for not only my dear,
ever-to-be-lamented brother—that dearest of all
my brothers—thought highly of my abilities;
but the most critical friends who had seen me
act, united in declaring that practice and perseverance alone were wanting to insure distinguished success. What happened at Canterbury
when the theatre fell into my hands, left me in
no manner of doubt as to the correctness of their
agreeable opinion; for, though quite out of
practice—not having played more than three

times during the previous three years—I enacted *Othello, Shylock, Earl Osmond, Hamlet,* and *Lord Hastings,* in a style the Canterbury judges thought very creditable. The press of that stupid city (like all other cities blessed with a cathedral peculiarly stupid), puffed me as though I had been all my life a great actor. To be sure—and I am bound to confess it—many of the critiques were written by myself; but, then, it is plain the editors would not have inserted them, if unconvinced they were based on the principle of judging righteous judgment. Certainly that flattering unction is very agreeable to my soul, whether agreeable to justice or not. I have often enjoyed a hearty laugh at these fine criticisms on my own performances, which no less than matter more important demonstrate how easily the world is gulled.

My speculation was a most unfortunate one. It is true I gained applause for my performances, and had the honour of puffing myself up in the Canterbury newspapers; but, then, I lost all my money. It was reported in a London newspaper (*The Era*) that after swindling the company, I " cut my stick," leaving my lodgings, &c., unpaid for. Report exaggerated considerably in that as in so many other cases. Undoubtedly I was unable at the time to pay the actors in full; but I gave to them an I.O.U., or promise to pay within a month of my return to London, which promise was faithfully kept. Theatrical people may doubt this. They may say such a tale is clearly apocryphal : because I believe mine is the first instance on record of a country manager having taken so extraordinary a course. Every member of the company received in full the sum promised. Never shall I forget the shout of mocking laughter and derisive scorn with which my proposal to give them I.O.U.'s for what remained due of their respective salaries was received. The truth is, these people decidedly agree with the author of "Tricks and Trials," who improves on Shakspeare by telling us "All the world's a *dodge*, and all the men and women merely *dodgers*." Knowing themselves dodgers, they naturally concluded that I was one. Nor did they conclude erroneously: for though I did them justice in the Canterbury affair—though I did *not* leave a host of people unpaid, as my personal enemy of *The Era* would have the world believe, I affect to be but a little more honest than my neighbours, and that they, yea, the very best of them, are *dodgers*, I am obliged to believe. None of us can afford to be much honester than the times we live in. The mouthing patriots and philosophical liberals who pretend to most of honesty, have generally the least to spare. They have their price, and would speedily be sold if "money-mongers" thought it worth their while to buy them. The pretension to disinterestedness put forth by these quack prescribers for all the ills which flesh seems heir to, is far more offensive than open bold-faced villainy. I make no such pretensions, and despise the egotistical braggarts who do. But, though no pretender to absolute honesty, I rather admire the quality—and on the failure of my theatrical speculation displayed more of it than I have since been given credit for.

CHAPTER XX.

INTERESTING INCIDENTS.

THE Canterbury affair cured me of a chronic affection for trying my luck in the lottery of theatrical management.   Up to the time when, like
certain out-at-elbows Thespians in " The Life
of an Actor," I flew by night from that dullest
of cathedral towns, my speculations had been invariably successful.   Then came the frost—the
killing frost—just too when I thought " full sure
my greatness was a ripening."   But though setting up " manager" emptied my purse, it did not
break my spirits—*nil desperandum* was my motto
—and immediately on my return to London I
contrived (though not without considerable difficulty) to get possession of the South London
Hall, corner of Webber-street, Blackfriars'-road
—a place well adapted for purposes of instruction or amusement, or both.   It flourished under
my direction : in other words the speculation
was a profitable one, notwithstanding the difficulty I then found in " saddling horses" with
that section of the Chartists who have a claim
upon the building.   Those claims are of a peculiar character, and by virtue of them it is at their
disposal on the Monday, Wednesday, Friday,
and Sunday evenings.   Had the building been
exclusively mine, I could have realized a heavy
sum in it.   As it was I did well.   The tenants
who preceded me disliked the Chartists, and the
Chartists disliked them.   Quarrelling was the order as well of the night as of the day.   The spirit
manifested was equal in intensity to that of the
hungry Kilkenny cats, and produced results no
less deplorable.   I succeeded in arranging with
my Chartist co-tenants for the delivery of lec-

tures in their hall every Sunday evening. The
terms were found mutually advantageous, and on
the same terms I continue regularly to lecture
for them every Sunday evening throughout the
year. It was whilst an occupant of the above-
named hall that I lost my second wife. She died
there after an illness of many months, during
which her sufferings were horrible in the extreme. Cancer of the uterus struck down in
the spring and vigour of life one of the kindest,
the most devoted and truthful of human beings.
It will perhaps be permitted me before finally
taking leave of this painful topic, again to assure
the reader that until I knew her I knew not the
power, the generosity, and wonderful devotion of
woman is capable. She lived to love, and for ~~which~~
the object loved or adored (for hers was a species
of adoration) she was prepared to go any length,
or make any sacrifice. Had my feelings been
equally ardent and sincere, we should have been
happy beyond measure. But they were not so.
I could not love this incomparable woman as she
ought to have been loved. I esteemed her
highly—sought to make her happy, *et voila tout.*
Our affections depend not upon ourselves. The
very defects of some appear more admirable in
our eyes than the noblest virtues of others. It
seldom happens that we most admire those who
are most worthy of admiration. And if intensely
loved by one whose affection we return but
coldly, or in part, the evil is greater than when
indifference is mutual. Cowley seems to have
thought the other sex too hot or too cold, or too
something that they ought not to be—at least so
I judge from the following lines :—

Hast thou not found each woman's breast (the land where
    thou hast travelled)
Either by savages possessed, or wild and uninhabited ?
Lust, the burning dog star, here rages with immoderate
    heat;
While Pride, the rugged northern bear, in others make
    the cold too great.
And where these are temperate found,
The rest is barren sand and rocky ground.

The difficulty Cowley found in obtaining a
woman precisely to his taste may be accounted
for without admitting the truth of this foul libel
on the other sex. Had he been fortunate enough
to meet with a woman whom he sincerely loved,
I doubt that he could have believed *too hot* the
willing object of his devotion, or as he fancifully
expresses it, that her breast was " by savages
possessed." Men rarely object to the warmth
of a woman, unless cold themselves. If we
complain of excess of affection *in* our wives, it
is because we have no superfluous affection *for*
our wives. A man who loves his wife never
can believe the affection of that wife as excessive, or deem it a bore. " I want not thee on
my neck," says the savage Orson, when Judith,
delighted at his return, flings her arms around
him. But Orson loved Judith much in the same
way that Master Bruin loves his she bear, or he
wolves at certain seasons love any wolf of the
softer sex. Newton, Bishop of Bristol, delighted
to speak of his marriage : and on one occasion,
after declaring it was the wisest thing he ever
did in his life, and that no wife could be better
than his, added—" She more than answered my
warmest wishes." The good divine did not mean
that his " dear" partner loved him too warmly.
Not a bit of it. He well knew it was impossible
for her to do that. What he meant was, that
he had a far more delightful companion than he
ever supposed she would be. When men complain that their wives are too fond, we may be
sure that their wives have good reason to complain that the complainers are not fond enough.
I most certainly was not fond enough of the wife
whose virtues I never shall cease to revere, and
whose untimely death I never shall cease to
deplore.

When this admirable woman passed from the
scene, and to mortal eyes became " ashes, a shade,
and a fable," I felt once more alone in the world.

She was eminently what is called a business woman. During her lifetime I had neither reason nor inclination to trouble myself about money matters. They were safe in her keeping, and I knew it. All confidence was reposed in her; nor do I believe that confidence was ever abused in a single instance. To marry again I had no desire. To carry on my business at South London Hall without a wife I found rather difficult, and very unpleasant. It happened, moreover, that about this time I got into trouble, or was pushed into it, by a set of thieves who do the work of certain functionaries with the style and title of Her Majesty's Commissioners of Inland Revenue. It had been my custom to furnish refreshment in the coffee room—chiefly coffee, tea, ginger beer, and other teetotal drinks. But many of my visitors, less virtuous, or less fastidious than teetotallers, desired to have beer or spirits, or both. I considered that if such articles were sent for when ordered, and no direct profit derived (the only charge made in such case being for use of hot water, attendance, &c.), no *legal* offence could be given to the excise worthies. They thought differently, and *in their peculiar way* sent me in a bill for £150; which I not being disposed to honor, determined to sell my business and go to America—a country I had often promised myself the pleasure of visiting. But as the wiseacres who know considerably more than *can* be known assure us, " There is a Providence which shapes our ends, rough hew them as we may." Before crossing the Atlantic I resolved once more to see France—*la belle France* —and to France I went. After enjoying myself at St. Cloud, Versailles, Rouen, and other places, I left Paris for Havre, a well-known sea-port, where I intended to take ship for the land of stars and stripes, which unquestionably is a land of liberty, because no one is denied the liberty of wolloping his own nigger. Luckily or unluckily, I know not which, the captain demanded £28 for my passage, a sum that seemed to me considerably more than I ought to pay, and I at once determined to go from Liverpool. On my way to that town I called at Manchester, chiefly for the purpose of seeing some old friends in that locality. On arriving there they induced me to take the well-known Hall of Science, Camp Field. Shortly after I published the *Lancashire Beacon*—carried on a free-thinking agitation unparalleled in that part of the country—and after a vain attempt to revolutionise Lancashire, settled down in London, where now I am, a hopeful though disappointed FREE-THINKER.

FINIS.

DIFFICULTIES OF CHRISTIANITY.

www.ingramcontent.com/pod-product-compliance
Lightning Source LLC
LaVergne TN
LVHW061220060426
835508LV00014B/1375

9 781535 812344